SACRED CONNECTION

Finding Our Path to Deeper Connection with Self and the Divine

CURATED BY ANN JONAS

Through The Center of Influence Community

Edited by Lil Barcaski and Kirsten Winiarski

Published by: GWN Publishing
www.GWNPublishing.com

Cover Design: Kristina Conatser

ISBN: 978-1-959608-62-2

CONTENTS

A Note From the Producer, 5

1) ROOT – ENERGY

ANN JONAS: *Love Is Everything!,* 8

2) SACRAL – CREATION

LINDSAY LEE: *Grace On Fire,* 26

3) SOLAR PLEXUS – EMBODIMENT

MICHELE LEEPER: *A Woman Reborn,* 50

4) HEART – VIBRATION

DR. JENNIFER MARKHAM, ND: *Be In Tune,* 64

5) THROAT – TRANSFORMATION

MAURINE XAVIER: *Breaking Open,* 84

6) THIRD EYE – INTUITION

BRENDA L BALDING RN, MA: *Sacred Discovery,* 106

7) CROWN – PRESENCE

ALICIA POWER: *The Sacred Art of Life,* 122

A NOTE
FROM THE PRODUCER:

I am honored to be introducing you, the reader, to this anthology. This book is an opportunity to bring into print form the essence of what started out as a nine-week collaborative, experiential webinar in October of 2022, the first round of *Sacred Connection.*

The incredible group of co-hosts, that have come into my energy field, ranging from a lifetime of connection to a first introduction, all were divinely led to participate. As we are amid the fifth round of this *Sacred Connection* journey, over 30 unique and amazing individuals have contributed their wisdom and magic. As a collective, the *Sacred Connection* Community, we are continuing to find our path to deeper connection with Self and the Divine.

When the connection was made and the opportunity for producing this book came into my reality, I jumped at the chance to write another chapter and this time do a deep dive into another aspect of my own unfolding journey. I began reaching out to find the co-authors that would be gathering together, here in Diving Timing.

I had intended for a book with nine chapters. The Divine had another plan. The six amazing Light-Minded Beings, that have joined me on this part of the *Sacred Connection* journey, are an incredible collection of wise and authentic Souls, that are walking the Earth with me as Love and Light Warriors.

As I was sitting with the meaning of seven chapters, I fell into the synchronicity of our body's seven chakra centers and found that each of our chapters fell beautifully into one of the energy centers.

As my chapter is foundational as Energy, meaning Love and God, the Root chakra as the base is a strong starting point. Then we move through the Sacral chakra with Lindsay Lee and her exploration into Creation, while Michele Leeper dances us through Embodiment in the Solar Plexus, power center chakra. The Heart chakra is where we breathe Vibration into our experience with Dr. Jennifer Markham and then Maurine Xavier will guide us through Transformation as an expression of the Throat chakra. Brenda Balding leads us into the realm of Discovery with Intuition as we pass through the Third Eye chakra and then we find our way into Presence with Alicia Power and the expansion through the Crown chakra.

I am so excited for what I am bringing to light, both in my chapter and in this whole anthology. The Center of Influence Community is providing a platform for the seven of us to share our messages, stories and wisdom. I recognize how serving our sacred connection has been and that this book will have an opportunity to now reach many more Light-Minded beings along their journey of Being in *Sacred Connection* with Self and the Divine.

As you roam through this book, may you find reflections of your own Magical journey, smiling back at you.

Offering love, light and hugs,

Ann Jonas
Curator and Producer of *Sacred Connection*

Dear Linda

My wish and intention for you is that you will always remember that the foundation of Everything is Love and that your journey here is as an expression of the Divine

Sending Love, Light and Hugs

[illegible] ☺

May these messages be serving

Ann Jonas

Ann Jonas, Transformational Guidance, is passionate about helping and supporting others to become more of who they truly are. She creates and holds space, in a safe container.

"My desire is to support soul/human beings in the unveiling of the higher self and allowing spirit to bring abundant happiness and love." ~ Ann Jonas

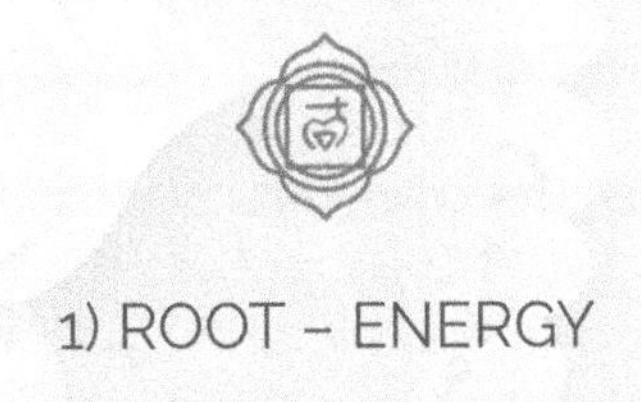

1) ROOT – ENERGY

LOVE IS EVERYTHING!

by Ann Jonas

FOUNDATION

Over the decades of my life's journey, there have been many different voices that have shared their truths. These voices have come from a variety of sources, and you may recognize some or all of which I'm about to offer in this chapter, as I share wandering thoughts and stories. One story has been repeated and every time I hear it OR tell it, I enjoy the "full body chills", the "God bumps" experience. There is this couple, with a 4-year-old and they have a second baby. A few months down the road, the child asks their parents if they could have some time alone with the baby in the crib. Not exactly sure how this young child of theirs might be feeling, the parents aren't sure if that's the best decision. They allow the visit and manage to still be within ear shot. It's what they hear that gets me every time, "Please remind me about God.... I'm starting to forget."

Why does that impact me so? Because I know that I and many other humans I know, have forgotten too. Also, it feels like the ultimate reflection of the reciprocal nature of God, reflected as spirit and traveling as human. Ok! Wait! Let's slow down and paddle out of this stream of consciousness, to a starting point.

There's a tale most everyone has heard in one way or another, about a person arriving at their next destination along the spiritual journey, that happens when their physical form dies. They are having a chat with God, taking a general scan of their life, noticing almost always there were two sets of footprints left behind. Yet as they looked more closely, during all the really hard parts there is only one set of footprints. They asked, "God, where were you when times were the hardest? Where did you go? I only see one set of footprints." God's response is, "That is when I was holding you. Those are my footprints you are seeing."

The latest version of myself, whom I lovingly refer to as Ann Jonas 3.0, has been revealed through peeling away another deep layer and witnessing myself on the next timeline of the spiral of life. I have full clarity about what I am here to offer as I have stepped into a *Sacred Connection* with my Self and the Divine. I am honored to share the stories of my life's experience. In some cases, there will be only a mention, a snippet, just a drop of deep, intense color, that will paint the picture of what I've navigated. As I offer this opportunity, by providing a mirror, I invite you to witness where there are reflections for you and your journey.

Foundationally, I exist with the awareness of two basic aspects and ways to be with what this life presents. **There is a basic purpose and a basic truth.**

- THE BASIC PURPOSE IS TO REMEMBER. We are here to remember why we came and understand that God is always present. It unravels and unfolds as we "happen" through the stories, the roller coaster rides, that make up the amusement park of our lives.
- THE BASIC TRUTH IS LOVE. It is the foundation of all. Love is Energy and Love is God. Love is Everything.

Here's the deal, Earth School is a 3rd dimensional reality that is based on polarity, meaning we have night and day, good and bad, right and wrong, light and dark. You get the picture. The thing is, it's all important and relevant for the structure of this reality.

It is what contains us. You know the movie *The Matrix*? Earth School is the place where we go to forget and then choose to find our way back and **Remember** that we ARE a Light Being. We are here expressing God Self as "Me", the Ann Jonas, and "You", (your name). We are all God, and this is what the 3rd dimensional reality offers us, a place to be expressed as God experiencing the human form, the human experiences of sensation and feeling. We express ourselves as the stories and identities of our lives so that we might come into this knowing.

"We are not human beings having a spiritual experience.
We are spiritual beings having a human experience."
— PIERRE TEILHARD DE CHARDIN

The magic happens when we decide to see outside the box and really KNOW God as the Universe, Love and All That Is. I know this through the choices in my life journey that guide me to random conversations or in-depth programs, to relationships or experiences that move through my life and offer me the opportunities to satiate my spiritual seeking, to bring everything from glimpses to full downloads, upgrades and opening. I am aware that it is always an energetic experience, unfolding along the way.

I will illuminate the places where I have come into clarity and made connections by sharing the stories of how I found my way, as I wander through what I now know to be a Divinely led life.

DEFINING LIFE MOMENTS

As I glance over the experiences of my life, many defining life moments have provided lessons, learning and growth and I'm grateful for all of them. It's the whole Lotus Path, there is no lotus without the mud. We all have life stories that are filled with trauma, tragedy, and all manner of "bad things happening". I am here to offer my way of seeing my experiences with the awareness that you always have a choice to have another perspective in your story.

As for stories and seeing other's perspectives, we all have a completely unique Energy signature, and no one has the same way of Being so what is relevant for my learning is not necessary for you and vice versa. Therefore, it is totally ridiculous to compare traumas or tragedies. Even if we experienced the same thing, each of us is going to have a different perspective. What's important to see is that we all have choice, no matter what the experience and everything has an impact in both polarities.

Two of the most defining moments of my life, that prepared me to Become me, were wrapped in the package of death, one instant and the other drawn out. The first one is surrounding my mother's exit from the planet, when I was 36-years old, by two bullets from a gun, held in the hand of my father, after they'd been divorced for 25 years. He went to jail and then joined my mother, back in the field of Loving Light, 18 months later.

The second package of death was a four-year roller coaster ride, with all kinds of turns and twists, with my partner of five years, along her melanoma journey, that led me to becoming a widow and single mom of a 2-year-old.

The community that I had built over my life began to form as a place for me to share our life updates and from there I was guided to write about what was being witnessed. I am here now to share the next iteration of my life through my writing, as I offer a perspective where I am allowing myself to keep coming out of the closet and offering the Lighthouse of my Voice and Presence to shine bright, loud, and clear.

> *"Then, one day, it clicks. The pain you had turns into peace as you accept that everything had to happen exactly as it did for you to be exactly who you are now. You hold no blame, bitterness, or resentment toward the experience, person, or yourself. Instead, you see it as the catalyst that led to your change and development. The very storm that shook so much in you also worked to clear your path."*
>
> — MORGAN RICHARD OLIVIER

Almost two years ago, on my 53rd birthday, I poked my head out of the vulnerability/shame closet and then I closed the door again. Eight months later, I found myself recognizing that expression was like the groundhog, I saw my shadow and went back in. It was at that point, about one year ago, having done another deep dive and received more clarity, that I flung open the closet, I was seeing the Light. I was ready to step out, to speak and share what had brought me to this point and how very timely it felt that my defense mechanisms were "falling away" as we were coming upon the Autumn Equinox.

I am writing this chapter now, in this anthology of *Sacred Connection*, and it is all due to this unfolding story, that occurred over the last year. The foundation of this story is based in some basic questions, that I feel I have learned how to answer and enjoy sharing my evolved clarity around.

I have come to learn there are many versions of God AND many ways to describe how, who, what, where and why God is. I'm in the deepest gratitude to know that I've come to realize that my whole life has been lived in the presence of a loving God and that I have come to a knowing that "I Am that I Am." This is an idea that allows us **to honor** that God is within us, **to know** that we are an expression of the Divine, as well as **to remind** us of the inherent, ever-loving nature of God.

It was July of 2022 and my partner and I, having been on a four-year journey, a roller coaster of epic proportions, had just decided to end our relationship. We came into this dynamic, as a power couple and that is relevant here, as we had a powerfully conscious uncoupling, still feeling like Soul family. We both recognize that our time together brought us to essentially the deepest, darkest, ugliest parts of ourselves, yet, as we are now more than a year beyond this completion, we are very much aware that it brought us clearly into the light as well. Nevertheless, in that moment, I was moving into a place where some might call a dark night of the soul.

I was at that point, like many on the planet, two years into the Covid lockdown situation when whatever work I had before, intuitive bodywork, and in-person retreats, workshops, and coaching, had essentially fizzled. I was looking for what was next. During this time, I had stepped into Shamanic work that sweetened all my life perspectives with the gifts and the medicine of the elements and brought to light the signs and synchronicities inherent in the natural world. Even with all of that, I was not inspired and didn't know where to look for answers.

One day, midafternoon, the sun's path offered its shining light, as it was passing over the roof of my house, beginning its descent towards the end of the day shining brightly through the west facing window of my bedroom. I found myself, there, lying in bed, watching fluffy white clouds float by, against the background of a beautiful blue sky, the periwinkle version. It was a gorgeous summer day, seen through the frame of the window, partially blocked by the slightly translucent curtains and the outside bushes. I was struggling with the fact that I had at least four decades of learning about tools and techniques, through therapy, coaching and workshops galore, not to mention books, movies, magazines, and podcasts. Yep, I'm a "Self-Help Junkie" living on "Earth School", and I know that Life is happening For us, Not To us. It's just the way it is.

(It's fun to find your way through your life choices, to understand more about who you are.)

Yet, in this moment, at this time, I was at a loss. I found myself wondering, at 53-years old, was this going to be my life or was I going to find my way back to joy. What I decided to do was to offer my dream time to the Divine. That night I asked my guides to provide me with guidance or a message while I slept, maybe a dream to remember upon waking. I'll be honest, I felt like I was taking the easy way out, the whole thing would happen while I slept.

The first night felt like a bust, nothing came through, but on the second night THEY woke me out of sleep and literally forced me to get the words out of my head. What came through was the idea for a newsletter, as the expression of me deciding that I am done WANTING to BE what I've WANTED to be in the world. It's time for me to Become all of me, sharing ALL my parts and truths. The other aspect of this amazing experience was a download that came through. It was the idea for a unique kind of workshop/webinar, something that I had never done, and it was to be called, "*Sacred Connection*". That night, I began a new chapter. The one that is Divinely led.

PARTS COMING TOGETHER

I remember a time in my twenties, in the beautiful and safe container of a women's community and workshop space where I felt as if I was standing on the precipice of a place where I could take off and fly. I have held that image throughout the evolution and awareness of my spiritual life, as a human in this lifetime, as I have come face to face with some of the darkest versions of myself, as well the most resilient. I have known the completely connected and deeply disconnected variations of myself and as it turns out, I've also met some really funny, very silly and totally goofy parts.

As I referenced earlier, when I was beginning to start down this Lotus Path, into the current version of the unfolding journey of the Spirit of who I Am, living as Ann Jonas, I spoke into it being and having some of the darkest points in my life. I was living front and center with the parts of me that had the faces and aspects of depression, laziness, addiction (in particular, to a device), self-deprecating ways of being, experiencing lack of self-worth, lack of self-love, even sometimes apathy.

All throughout these energetic qualities, were layers of fear. Even in the darkest times though, I was never at a point of no return. I always knew that the sun would rise again, just like it does day after day. I knew that Winter would become Spring. Even though, like a hologram on a spaceship, IT FELT REAL in all ways. I began to find the synchronicities and recognize that there were threads of all these emotions, woven through my life and relationships.

What I saw happening was that I was caught in a fear cycle, with ideas of looking like a fraud or having feelings of inadequacy, I felt stuck. Yes, in the Mud. What seemed most disconcerting is that this appeared self-created. I allowed myself to step into what started feeling like quicksand, the more I struggled against myself, the more I sank. Who am I to stand up and offer my Knowing? What makes me so special? A lifetime of self-development guided me to ask a different kind of question, one that references Marianne Williamson from *Our Deepest Fear*, "Who am I not to be?"

I have been yearning for this point in my journey when I would be brave enough to really show up as ALL of me, not knowing exactly what that would look like. The parts and aspects of me that are filled with light and love, resilience, trust, and a deep desire to hold and support others are in existence when I'm coming from **Love** and not Fear. I celebrate how connected I am when this part is front and center.

I know we all have parts, so I offer you some questions to ponder:

- Do I recognize my parts?
- How do I navigate AS my parts?
- What parts feel front and center?
- What parts do I choose not to share?

As I believe to be true, all things happen for a reason, and they occur in Divine Timing and Alignment. We find the paths that bring us our teachings and our growth opportunities along the way. As the universe designed, I was scheduled for a session with a psychic medium that I'd worked with before. This day turned out to be filled with deep emotional release followed by powerful synchronicities. Through the lenses of my guides and angels, I was reminded that since I was a 2-year-old, I have been showing up in the world based on survival techniques. What became clear is that my perception of the energetically unsafe space I was in at that point in my life set me up to equate control with safety. A pivotal experience was that I got a brother, but he had some hard times in the beginning so more attention to him was important and necessary yet created some challenging experiences for my parents to navigate. Then six months later, my dad checked himself into a mental facility. This marked the beginning of his mental illness impacting my life in incredibly traumatic ways. I am painfully aware that my coping mechanism, in response to this incredible feeling of instability, since all things seemed to be in chaos, was that I chose to decide to be in control of my environment, at all times, and this would keep me safe.

In essence, what I feel I discovered is that I've only felt "safe" when I'm in control of my experiences. I have "known" of this for decades as I have been peeling away the layers but this time, this layer allowed me to see that when the control is not there and I let down my defenses, I feel vulnerable. That vulnerability I've come to recognize was not something that I was willing to allow so I kept building more features on the control panel and "keeping it all together". This, I believe, is how the parts came to be. I love the way the Pixar movie *Inside Out* portrayed these different parts. I highly recommend a viewing, even without kids.

In addition to the Big Reveal of my vulnerability and the ways that I seem to hold myself back as I've created these safety nets, this session also gave me a Big Thumbs up for allowing myself to recognize how I am now READY to let go. I came home and was called to pull an oracle card from Rebecca Campbell's *Work Your Light* oracle deck and as I love to say when it comes to divine guidance, "You can't make this shit up."

The card I pulled is entitled "Leap" and the message is:

> *"You go first. The Universe will catch you. Life bends for the courageous. The Universe wants to support you, but first you need to leap. To throw your life up in the air. Perhaps you know what you are being called to leap toward (or away from) but are scared to make the move. Or maybe perhaps you are waiting for a big fat sign or instruction manual, or permission to do so first. If this is*

you, then this card is your sign and permission slip to take a deep breath and leap into the unknown. It's scary to let go of all that we know in hope for something new. And it's normal to feel anxious at the thought of letting go of what we know for sure. But this is the unavoidable process of rising. And right now, this is how you are being called to live.

"Nature is constantly showing us how to live with courage. Fall comes every year and encourages the trees to loosen their grip. To allow what once was so full of life, to fall away, leaf by leaf. For a moment, it feels like nothing will grow again."

As I allowed for what was falling away and took the leap, I imagined the experience of falling leaves, releasing at the point where the connection to what's holding them to the branch, isn't strong enough anymore. There is a release and then it falls, without attachment, without grasping. I witnessed how I was letting go and allowing for the ways that bring me *Sacred Connection*.

My **reason** for sharing this, whether it's on my website, in a newsletter or here in this chapter, is my desire for deeper connection through vulnerability, creating a framework and foundation for how I've arrived at this place. My desire is to contribute to others finding their own ways of *Sacred Connection*. As I mentioned earlier, I was literally given a download of something to offer as a Teaching. Yes, I've done workshops and retreats, but this offering is a unique combination of conversation, collaboration, community, creativity, and the beginning of an unfolding journey.

The first 9-week series began mid-October and ended at the Winter Solstice. It only made sense to begin another round and now, at the writing of this chapter, we are starting the fifth round and second year of *Sacred Connection* and growing the community through the *Sacred Connection* Community Portal. Over the time since I began this journey, I completely shifted my life with a move out of California and as a result The *Sacred Connection* Sanctuary and Retreat Space was birthed and co-created.

DIVINE MOMENTS

All of this has been Divinely led. In fact, my whole life has been Divinely guided and I'm now, at 54-years old, feeling immense clarity about life and totally aware of the guidance and support that I have received to allow for all of this to come to light and manifest into Being. I invited in the path and trusted that it would be serving in the highest regard of what I could envision, or something better. I trusted in a lifetime of knowing that had been expressed as doing the "manifestation work" of writing down things on nice paper, meaning that if I really wanted it to come into being, I would honor some aspect of ceremony or ritual.

This brings us to the exploration of God, as It has shown up in my life.

In early May of this year, I found myself posting a meme on Facebook, with this message: "I trust in Diving Timing. The Universe always has my back." I was in the depths of a massive shift in my life, to sell my house, buy a different one and move out of the only state I'd ever called home. What to some seemed impossible only translated to me as "I'm possible." Not only was all of this possible, it was also meant to be. My whole life has been that way. What I was witnessing unfold was a retroactive awareness that I have always been seeking the answer to the question. "What is my relationship with God?"

This is something that I have always known, somewhere deep inside. Yet, I didn't always follow my heart or really "allow" myself to trust in that unknown thing and divine timing. I didn't even trust in what I understood God to Be.

My journey to God began as I was born a Hayman, in a reform Jewish home. My parents met at a B'nai B'rith dance and once they were ready for kids, six years later, they made the decision to join a temple and do right by the kids, raise them Jewish and I guess that meant with God. The funny thing I remember though, when I think about that part of my journey is that in the prayer books, they wouldn't even spell out the whole word, it was "G-d". There was something about God being so separate from us that we couldn't spell his name. I'll be honest, I'm still not sure what that was all about, nor do I need an answer. It was not a bad life. Sunday school and temple on Fridays sometimes. Otherwise, it was Sabbath at home with the candles and the prayers. Eight days of Hanukkah and I always loved the food, still do and I make some of the best Latkes, everyone who has eaten them will tell you. Anyway, around 11 years old, I started preparing for my Bat Mitzvah and then my home fell apart, when my parents got divorced. I wondered a lot where God was then.

Mom left the temple, found the Baha'i Faith and then it was still God but from a different perspective. I was still intent on having my Bat Mitzvah at 13, which I did and then joined the Baha'i journey with my declaration of my faith in Baha'u'llah at the age of 15. It just made sense. Plus, we happened to be in Israel at the time, visiting my Bubi, my mom's mom, who lived and worked in Haifa, supporting the Seat of the Universal House of Justice, the center of the Baha'i Faith. It was a pretty cool thing to get to sign my Declaration card in such an auspicious location. I like things like that.

I turned my back on all of that at 16, when I found myself not being "the good girl" and breaking all the rules so none of it made sense anymore. Arriving in my 20s, I was discovering a completely new path to God or in this case Goddess. I was taking the Composition 101 class that has THE research paper, where you can pick any topic that you like. Well, my thoughts were, "I believe in witches." Sure enough, I was pleasantly surprised to find many books referencing: Wicca, Paganism and Goddess Religion. In my way of seeing it, this expanded my experience of Religion to a sense of Spirituality, that continued to unfurl over the next 30 years.

Looking back, I see some of the choices I made were with the KNOWING that I would be supported. Other decisions where my trust and confidence wavered were due to fear and feeling vulnerable or losing control. I feel like I went rogue and "forced" things into being, often creating some uncomfortable outcomes.

Moving through life, dipping in and out of believing in and trusting that there IS something and witnessing how the world felt about God, in all its different ways, I had to discover for myself the meaning behind God and what is Religion vs Spirituality. How are they different and what is the same? Where is God coming from, with all those different messages? I was so curious. The learning came in fits and spurts, as I connected with various teachers along the way, in all forms.

Then a big learning and a massive shift came, with a bang. There was that one night, when I learned the truth for me and was led to the answer by Divine Intervention. My mom was up visiting me, we were having dinner out, when I lived in the Mission district of San Francisco. It was a powerful night, and the memory is still there, in all of my senses. I can smell the Indian food wafting all around me, feel the texture of the brocade fabric covering the cushions underneath my legs, as we were sitting on stone benches. I hear the dishes and glasses clanking as conversations are swirling in the space. I see the lights of the cars passing by, through the floor to ceiling windows, creating glowing shadows, dancing with color, all around the room.

I was in my early thirties and had been in a few relationships with women over the last 10 years. She was always super cool about my girlfriends and embraced them all as family but on this night, in this conversation, she uttered the words, "Based on the laws of nature, this is a 'spiritually diseased' relationship." There was nothing in me that accepted that as true and if this was her God, I needed none of him, so I said, "Well, I don't believe in God anyway!" I swear to God, I'm not fucking kidding I heard a thunderclap in my head. At that moment, I remember almost looking up and saying that I was sorry but that I was in an argument with my mother and that I couldn't back down.

Anyway, as we always did, things smoothed over and dinner went on peacefully. Now it was time to go to see a movie. The movie we were planning on we were "running late for", so we grabbed one of those free newspapers (remember there weren't phones or internet at this time) and it sent us to a theater for a movie that we were curious about, yet the theater was not only closed but it had a chain around the door handle. Around the corner though was another theater showing only one movie, starting in those few moments, and we thought the actors might be interesting, so we got into our seats. The movie's opening scene is a funeral, and the story is all about a young boy in his search for the meaning of life and where his grandfather went. For me this was a search for God and an answer for me. In that simultaneous moment, both my mother and I placed our hands on each other's legs and squeezed, in a loving acknowledgment of the truth and how we were led there.

CONNECTION

From that moment on, I was open to all the ways that I received information. Whether it looked like intuition, gut instinct, protective thoughts, or inner knowing, I was given multitudes of opportunities to "test" out the validity of these messages and find out the hard way when I would sometimes dismiss their importance.

Whatever you want to call it: God, Goddess, Love, Divine, Source, Energy, Mystery, Universe. It doesn't matter what the word is, it's all the same. Through this understanding, we can answer those five little questions that we are all so familiar with when it comes to seeing the whole picture:

- **Who** is God?
- **What** is God?
- **Where** is God?
- **Why** is there a God?
- **How** is God experienced?

I am going to answer all of these questions with one statement:

God is a Guiding Support that is Love and Energy, existing in Everything and desiring to experience life through our expression. It is seen in our lives that when we Trust, Surrender, Let Go and let the Divine lead, that we are experiencing God as ourselves and we are also showing the world and contributing to the collective field our understanding and relationship with All That Is.

Once I seemed to have a handle on God, I felt like I had to reclaim the word since so many are uncomfortable with it for a multitude of reasons. It felt great to be "Good with God" and then I had to figure out the difference between Religion and Spirituality.

In essence, what I have distilled it down to is Religion provides three beautiful things:

- Community of like-minded people
- Structure, moral code, a life of ethics
- The "ways" or "means" to access God

Spirituality has all of those things AND the freedom to practice as you see fit. What it DOES NOT HAVE are the aspects of Religion that are fear-based, punitive, restrictive, exclusive, and generally dogmatic.

This is the place where people are fighting or killing, in the Name of God.

As I glance back at the spiral I have traveled, I see how I have exponentially increased my ability to trust. Witnessing myself as I float through the narrowest point, trusting that I will slip right through, whatever it is that I encounter, I am supported all the way. I know that God and the Universe always have my back.

Sacred Connection, in some ways, is the ultimate expression of my life's journey. It's how I have come to embrace this life, as well as honor Divine guidance and support. I am honored to be curating and facilitating this collective space and growing community as we dance in the themes of *Sacred Connection* that are holding us, like the chapters in this book.

I invite you to come out with your Spiritual Self and you will find that the mirrors of yourself will be seen in the ones that see you, as a reflection of God.

Every one of us has an experience around our journey towards and away from God.

I'm curious:

How does my story resonate for you? What parts of my life journey reflect your stories?

> *"I help people as a way to work on myself, and I work on myself to help people... To me, that is what the emerging game is all about."*
>
> —RAM DASS

My mess has always been my message and we are all here to learn from each other. I receive the utmost joy from supporting others to see their own Light and Divinity, amidst the pain and challenges of life. I am honored to walk the path of Transformation.

I invite you to connect with me about joining this journey. The spiritual seeking path of Being connected to Self and the Divine, here in The *Sacred Connection* Community.

Lindsay Lee

Lindsay is an embodiment coach empowering women to reconnect with their bodies. Facilitating how to create safety with and for your body. She offers insight and intuitive perspective for deep connection and growth. An artist and mystic, dancer and dreamer, healer and healed. She facilitates healing inner child wounds and encourages you to step into your best self.

2) SACRAL – CREATION

GRACE ON FIRE

by Lindsay Lee

NO ONE STARTS FROM NOTHING

But the universe will level you out if need be.

In mythology, the phoenix is described as an immortal bird that cyclically regenerates. It began as a common bird who's nest was set on fire by the hand of a god-like figure. As the fire consumed the bird, instead of suffering, she decided to dance in the flames.

Ultimately, the fire reduced the bird to ashes and instead of blowing away in the wind, she was reborn and arose from the pile of ash to begin again.

So, there I was sitting in my living room while the flames of metaphorical disaster consumed me. It was 2017 and my then husband was sitting starry eyed across from his girlfriend. The way he smiled at her… *when was the last time he slightly looked at me that way?* No, this was not an open marriage. There were some serious boundaries crossed and this "meeting" was to show me that they were meant to be together, or something like that. I had to say to myself, "No, Lindsay, this isn't a movie, this is really your life."

When he told me he wanted to be with someone else, I dropped to the floor and felt myself give up. I put SO much energy into that relationship only to be met with avoidance and an emotional wall that literally had me questioning if he was on the spectrum. When she showed up, I realized what I had been putting energy into, an energetic vacuum.

I could stay in the victim story of, "he left me." However, when I was honest with myself, I realized I had subconsciously prayed for a way to get out of this mediocre relationship, I just didn't realize it. I remember I was sweeping the kitchen floor and praying about our relationship. "Help this man to let me in. Help our relationship improve. Help our communication to get better. Help our connection…" (On and on, I listed qualities I wished for in our relationship.) I got to the end of my prayer and I said, "That or something better."

It was like someone shook the dust out of a blanket. I felt the "shoom" or flicking of the vibration that shifted the very foundation from under me. I remember thinking, *"what was that?"* This shift was peculiar and it made me pause. I continued to sweep, but I knew something had changed.

It was only a matter of months since that prayer when he so coldly said to me, "I want to be with her. It's always been her." And I knew it was done. It was easier for him to let her in than to let me in after years of showing him I was a safe person.

He didn't want to be married and I knew that deep down. I heard an inner whisper and I ignored it. The voice that was there as I cried myself to sleep, over and over again, throughout our relationship. I shoved it down. I had devoted so much time and energy to this person, I was determined to make it work. But he found every excuse to push me away and I always wondered why. No matter how much I showed up, he still had a wall.

A few months before we got married, I offered him an "out." I said to him, "You don't seem excited to get married." After nine and a half years in a relationship (including 5 years of marriage), he didn't have the capacity to articulate what he was thinking, which was something along the lines of, "Linds, we want different things in life. We should separate." Instead, he abruptly moved her in, and waited for me to move out. Thankfully a friend allowed me to stay with her while I searched for an apartment to move into. Our relationship crumbled in a rapid and traumatizing manner, yet even in the worst moments, part of my soul knew this situation was unfolding for my highest good.

The phoenix chose to dance in the flames and rebirth herself into something new. The power in choosing to create out of chaos is one that many artists understand.

Even though I knew the foundation in my marriage wasn't stable, I tried so hard to make it so, and the shift in this part of my life was massive. The chaos of that foundation that crumbled in flames left me feeling woozy, displaced, and shaken. I went through a period of time of not trusting anyone.

TRANSMUTING THE SACRED SHIT / THE ART OF SURRENDERING

"I have no creativity. I can't even draw a stick figure." I hear this all the time when I tell people I'm an artist. My response is almost always something like, "Well, yes you can, and being an artist is a taught skill. It's whether or not you want to drive your passion and energy into expanding that skill."

It only takes a few seconds to see how that react to my comment for me to decipher if they will be responsive to my coaching to unleash their inner artist. If they pause and receive my message, the conversation (and subsequently, our creative working relationship) flourishes. If they are unwilling to recognize that they can, in fact, draw a stick figure, that creativity is so much more than they're believing, we almost always part ways.

If they aren't receptive to my invitation to be create, I do not judge them. The creative discourse perishes and we move onto carrots and whatever fun dip is being served at whatever gathering we're at.

Creating art is a taught skill, like riding a bike, or baking. There are certain steps to take and you can achieve a certain outcome. Being an artist requires a different kind of surrender that most people only skim the surface of. But we witness such greatness in artists like filmmaker Denis Villeneuve, actor Viola Davis, writer and poet Maya Angelou, or singer/songwriter, and now actor, Lady Gaga. We allow creativity and chaos within their works of art to be placed on pedestals because they are well known and well paid.

But what we forget is that as children we all had glorious imaginations that took us to the moon. As we danced among butterflies and ran barefoot in the grass, we imagined entire worlds with great super powers.

Children have this immense capability of being open, curious with wonder, and have an insatiable appetite to discover the world.

When did we stop? Why did we stop? More importantly, why did we close ourselves to curiosity and rediscovering life?

I was 13 when I consciously made the decision to pursue a career in the arts. School did not come easily to me and art making was quite honestly one of the few places where I felt safe. Hell bent on becoming a professor, so I could teach people how to follow and trust their creative intuition and listen to their inner whisper, I made sure my resume was packed with credentials to back my knowledge, intuition, and skills. But like many life path goals, life and honestly the institution of academia got in the way. My higher-self forged a divine redirection, and I was brave enough to hear the call (quite frankly catapulted) and then surrender to the voice coming from within me.

The act of creation is inherently feminine. Creative individuals receive an idea and then make something of it with whatever method they are drawn to. Academia has masculinized this process and is more interested with how much work you're making and showing. I witnessed so many colleagues making art on fumes. No judgement, they're being pulled in so many directions and burning out.

How does one even begin on allowing themselves to surrender for creativity to flourish? You have to admit you're hearing an inner whisper. If you're in denial you won't get very far. It requires the ability to let go and get out of your own way. If you don't, God or the Universe will absolutely hit you with a 2x4.

Letting go and surrendering is usually easier said than done. Right?

One of my first major 2x4's, where I actually began to listen to my inner whisper, was the break-up of my marriage. I know it happened because the Universe decided I was strong enough to handle the blow. Not only creatively but also as a woman. I was really beginning to heal on deep levels and suddenly the patterns I noticed we were in, were absolutely not working for me.

When you're pushing for growth and your partner isn't, it creates a deep discord between you that is unavoidable. This is why *growing together* is important in relationships.

In regards to the creative spirit, it's through practice that we understand how to surrender to the subtle whisper within. I say all the time (I'm sure I'm quoting someone) that artists are the antennas to the transcendent other. We receive an idea, trust it, and then empower ourselves to go create it. This is a glorious dance with the Divine.

There's a point within each art class I've taught where the students "zone out" and are in the act of making. There's barely any side chatter, the room gets quiet, and all you hear is charcoal scraping on the paper, or hammers and chisels gouging away at blocks of plaster. I've noticed that hair stylists also do this. They get quiet with whatever conversation their in and "get in the zone" as they cut or color hair. This is them surrendering to the process.

Why is this needed? No one ever made anything great while they were stressed. There might have been a stressful event that was a catalyst to spark their decision to create, but while making, there is some level of relaxation and surrender. It is a way of channeling all their skills and creative energy.

Art making is not for the weak minded. It demands a level of perseverance that a lot of people cave into their desire for immediate gratification. This in itself is surrendering, acknowledging that there's a gap between where you are with the level of skill you currently have and your taste. This is good. Your level of taste will propel you into a work ethic that will keep you hungry and pushing for more. If you stay open and curious you will allow yourself to check more than one box for what method you choose from for your desired creative endeavors.

Meaning, if you stay open and curious, you won't get locked into one method and say, "I'm a painter so all I do is paint," but you will in fact allow yourself to say, "I'm going to explore what cooking will do for me and my creative spirit today and paint another day." Or replace cooking with writing, singing, dancing... you get the point.

What does it take to surrender? Like I mentioned earlier, you need to relax. If you've had anyone snap the word "relax" at you in a dismissive way, this word can be confusing and somewhat triggering. Don't sweat it, I've been there, I got you.

Take a moment to focus on your breathing. Close your eyes and notice how you're taking in air. Almost always, this exercise in awareness causes people to instinctually then take a deeper inhale. If you just did this, congratulations. We now know you're holding your breath and not breathing enough for your body and brain to get the much needed oxygen.

Ok great, now what? Allow yourself to take deeper breaths and find a rhythm with this. If you're now yawning as a result, it's just your brain catching up from being deprived of oxygen. With this new found awareness, I encourage you to prolong your exhales. This will calm your nervous system even more and allow you to begin the process of surrendering. This space of surrender will allow you to begin to feel what you're avoiding and to hear your inner voice.

When you're in a relaxed state, you're more likely to be receptive and surrender into a state of flow with whatever task you're working on.

THE ART OF MAKING

I remember walking on Main Street in Moscow, Idaho. It was a particularly tough night of hardly sleeping. I woke up about 2AM. I sat up abruptly, grabbed my chest, and cried until it was time to muster my way to class. I still had one semester left of grad school and by this point I had only been living at my new place away from my husband for a couple weeks. I remember telling myself, "It's shit like this that make a great artist."

But I am so done with the suffering artist narrative. I've never been one to create *while* I'm in the shit storm, but only as a way of reflecting and processing what I've been through.

In one of the many fights proceeding our breakup, my ex was overcome with anxiety about how I'd be making art about what was happening, about how he was treating me. I said with ultimate truth in my voice, "You're damn right I will." Knowing that art was more than just painting or using material in a visual way to articulate a concept, I knew I would write and share my story.

My intention is not to shame him. I share my story as a vehicle to talk about perseverance and how to navigate shit storm after shit storm.

How many partners devote their lives to their romantic other only to be dropped when things get tough? Goldie Hawn said something like, "Women who are financially free are free in every aspect of their lives because they aren't dependent on a man." A lot of women are waking up and getting creative with generating income. Freeing themselves and taking a good look at the relationships they find themselves in.

I digress, back to walking to class in Moscow. I remember trying to reason with myself about how I can still have the same dream, it would just look a bit different now. *New beginnings are new art projects, I get to try new things and create a level of safety that was meant for me.* I tried to slip into the same vibration of starting a new art project, with the same level of excitement and curious spirit.

Logically, every fiber within my being said, *this is for the better*. But there were definitely moments where I would fight for the marriage. (The ego tends to go back to what is familiar.)

It's ok. The little girl inside me was terrified. Even with some inner child healing the abandonment wound was still taking over and I was feeling so lost. It would be two years before I felt a glimmer of inspiration again.

How do you surrender in the face of deep grief?

For me, it's a way of connecting deep within and finding the vibration of truth. It's a physical sensation deep in my gut and trusting it. Even if I don't fully understand what it means yet, I follow that sensation. Having had so much practice as an artist, and listening to my creative instincts, I get to exercise this practice in real life now.

They say it takes about half the time of your relationship length to get over someone. Yes, and no. Because we were so enmeshed in each other's lives, it was difficult on an energetic level to imagine my life any other way. But also, I have a type of personality that will mourn the relationship along the way if I'm paired with someone not meeting me halfway. We were roommates that slept in separate beds which were on the floor next to each other. How in the world was I okay with this kind of life? Truth is I wasn't. In fact, this and other intimacy issues were the center of my dissatisfaction. The cyclical conversations around intimacy was always abruptly ended because he felt attacked and unable to actually have a dialogue. I was breadcrumbed with future promises, and when I began to refuse to let him off the hook, he became uncomfortable. I could see the panic in him as I became stronger.

Movies like, "He's Just Not That Into You," come to mind as a flag of, *Hey, pay attention here. There's a message reflective of what's going on in your life.* (Inner whisper!) And when I would point that out to my ex, he gaslit me and made to believe that I was the crazy one. I was too emotional. I was too imaginative. I was too… fill in the blank here because his finger pointing excuses went on and on.

Somewhere along the line, I had to get off the neutral fence and stand up for myself in a bold way. To use my God given fire and passion in a way that would make sense for my life. I get to create my life from this place.

After Moscow, I spent some time in New Jersey and ended up taking care of my grandmother while going through the divorce. I found a teaching position at Rutgers University and a part-time job in retail.

And the empowering viewpoint of that situation is that I got to give back to a woman (my grandmother) who gave so much to her family. Is she a difficult woman? Yes. And the truth is she is unable to untangle her trauma and emotions. No wonder it manifested into dementia.

I also got to support my mom while she had surgery. I found purpose as a caregiver but also recognized the issue in that scenario. Sitting on the couch with my mom and grandmother I had a huge lightbulb moment. I recognized we all had broken hearts. We all have L names. And we were all a little lost.

My mother did the best she could with what she knew how to do. Is she a difficult woman? Yes. And the truth is she is laced with trauma and unable to untangle her emotions. (Do you see a pattern?) Me too. Of course, everything was complicated. Of course, I found myself in another entangled mess with a parent who wouldn't listen. (Do you see another pattern?)

While on that couch I had a vision of helping women detangle their emotions, take down their guards, lean into vulnerability, and help empower them. I just didn't know how yet.

After the divorce was finalized, I took a job teaching in South Carolina. I loaded my little red Ford Focus up with ALL my belongings and drove down on New Year's Day so I wouldn't hit any traffic. When I arrived, I went up and down the stairs with full arms more times than I remember to count, and felt an immense amount of relief as I unpacked the mattress from a box. I remember breathing a little deeper as it puffed up with air.

As I laid down, exhausted in this new, unfurnished apartment with unfamiliar smells and new sounds, I remember feeling that little girl inside sensing some fear.

I curled up in my blanket and said to myself, *now I get to start this new adventure. I get to create my life and really start living.*

Or so I thought…

THE KID STOLE GOD'S SCRIPT

When the pandemic hit, I remember seeing a meme about how a little kid clearly stole God's script and with a crayon was writing "and then an invisible monster took away everybody's smell and taste, and then everyone got diarrhea and all the toilet paper disappeared from the stores..."

I wasn't at my new location for more than two months when everything shut down because of COVID. I didn't know anyone and I wasn't near family. I had only just bought a couch and felt super proud that I was furnishing my new place and that I was doing it on my own.

Suddenly, my work load tripled. Students were freaked out, and I somehow turned into everyone's counselor. (A trend that tends to happen for female instructors.) That was okay, because I was totally alone and had all this free time anyway, right?

No.

As the semester ended, I found a part time gig at Lowe's Home Improvement and trusted that this would carry me through the summer until I started teaching again. Because an adjunct professor's salary is worse than a teacher's salary for K-12.

July of 2020, the day before my birthday, I was headed to a celebration dinner with a friend of a friend (because I still really didn't have any in my new found location and wanted to celebrate my birthday.) I was in the left lane and the light was green ahead. Suddenly this mini-van in the center lane turned left, not far from me, into a shopping center causing me to slow down. I remember thinking, *wow that was close why didn't they just wait?* And then, out of seemingly nowhere this SUV type vehicle pulled out from the same shopping center in front of me with the intention of turning left.

I slammed on my brakes. There was absolutely no way I wasn't going to hit them. AND this was the longest few seconds of my life. My brain said to my body, *relax*. No, I screamed at myself in my head, *RELAX!* And, apart from my foot still on the brakes, I dropped my body, exhaled, and did my best to do this thing... relax.

And then. Nothing.

When I came to, I thought my car was on fire. It was the smoke from all the airbags and I was panicked. I was trying to open my door. I looked up and saw the crack in my windshield and I was really confused about it. *What just happened? Why do my teeth hurt? Where am I? I couldn't open my door, why can't I open the door?!?* My movements echoed the panic inside. The airbags from the door were in the way so I climbed over to the passenger side desperate to get out.

A man who saw the whole thing crossed the street and told me to stay where I was. He grabbed my hand and I said to this man shaking, "My name is Lindsay, please don't leave me." He helped calm me down and talked to the dispatcher who suddenly was on my car speakers. I remember thinking, *thank you technology.*

I remember being asked by the medics if I wanted to go to the ER and my thought was, *yeah I don't have a ride home now.* And then, I distantly thought of Liam Neeson's wife Natasha Richardson who died from a head injury. "I should probably get checked," I told them.

When I got to the ER, I was adamant about asking for a concussion screening, I remember feeling nauseous while getting an x-ray of my wrists that I was convinced were broken and I remember a friend of a friend picking me up from the ER.

I didn't know what went into a concussion screening. As far as I knew, I had never had one before, so I had no idea how long it would take to recover. Turns out I wasn't given one. And it wasn't until my third return to a different ER that I was finally diagnosed with one.

All the physicians said it takes a while. I was going to physical therapy thinking, this is normal. I was trying to convince myself that what I was experiencing was normal.

I was taking Ubers everywhere on my limited adjunct professor budget and trying to book appointments in close proximity to each other so I could walk from one location to the other. I would Uber to physical therapy in the morning, walk across the street to the chiropractor who was conveniently located next to a Walmart, go grocery shopping at Walmart, and then Uber home. All while navigating vertigo, memory loss, dizziness, trouble walking, trouble talking, numbness in most of my body, trouble focusing cognitively, trouble focusing with my eyesight, numbness and loss of function in my hands to name a few symptoms.

It wasn't until I saw a specialist back in Philly who told me, "We're out of concussion territory now, we're in Traumatic Brain Injury." There was something in me that just knew it. I could sense my doctors at home frustrated that I wasn't getting better on their schedule and no one thought it was more than the initial diagnosis. They were quick to dismiss me, unwilling to help or even care.

I mean, I knew not being near anyone who could help me keep tabs on my progress was an issue. But at this point I was eating only with my hands for more than four months because I wasn't able to hold silverware. The brain fog I was experiencing was SO thick I don't know how I was still able to teach. Aside from studying art since I was 13, it was in my bones and second nature to me. Every ounce of my exhausted energy was focused on any conversation I was trying to have. Quite frankly the thoughts weren't even solid enough to come down through my mouth for me to articulate what I wanted. I was saying only what I could say and not what I wanted to say. And two seconds into any conversation I was forgetting what we were talking about.

And then, I got COVID from an Uber driver. How in the world did I not see that I was being redirected by God here? Remember earlier, I was *hell bent* on becoming a professor? I was stubbornly determined and still lectured with a TBI and COVID. (Insert strange facial expression here, no worries I'm doing it for you.)

It wasn't until January 2021 that I started driving again. Still in physical therapy, we were doing everything to get me to a status of almost normal for basic life functions. (Like putting a key into a door, walking upstairs without feeling like I needed to vomit, buttoning my shirt, following a moving target with my eyes.) When classes started back in person I was putting ALL my effort into appearing normal. No one had any idea how much effort I was really devoting towards this and I would crash whenever I'd get home.

Oh, and fun fact, in March I realized my boyfriend at the time was actually not who he said he was. (Another book, I assure you.) Why is this random fact relevant? I sat on the couch in disbelief for three days straight at the shit show that was unfolding in my life. *How in the world did I get here?*

I got up after day three and hired a therapist. I've been through some stuff before but this was out of my league of personal development. I needed help and knew it. I told her about the meme I saw about the pandemic. I joked that the kid who stole my script was doped up on sugar, scribbling with a red crayon all over Lindsay's life with "AND THEN her husband decided to be with a mutual student of theirs, AND THEN she took care of her grandmother while going through a traumatic divorce, AND THEN got into a car accident AND got a traumatic brain injury, AND THEN she got COVID, AND THEN she found out her boyfriend is lying to her about who he was, AND THEN, AND THEN, AND THEN."

"I feel like taking the crayon away from this child saying firmly, 'and now you're done with the crayon. No more 'AND THEN!'"

At least I can joke about it, right? And that's what I did. I metaphorically took crayon away. I quit my job and moved again.

THE MAGICIAN AND THE WORKER BEE, NOW THE REAL WORK BEGINS

When the Universe hits you over and over again, it's time to listen. I had absolutely no choice but to surrender.

No amount of determination and perseverance can withhold you from your Divine plan. Believe me, I tried and look how well that worked out.

When I moved after quitting academia, I was triggered with so much grief. And once again I had no direction of where to take my life because I didn't really allow for another consideration of what to do. I was truly starting over at a whole new baseline. But like I talked earlier about childlike curiosity and the need to stay open, I had to figure out a way to calm my nervous system and create safety so I could play in creativity again. One step at a time. However slowly, each step was (metaphorically and literally), I was grateful I was taking the step.

Emotions that come up in big waves, I simply sit and allow them to. I assign myself a seat and say, *okay, this is my safe space to release whatever comes up for however long it needs to be purged. And I will sit here until I'm complete with this.* I breathe as the waves hit me over and over again. Flooding to the surface seemingly without control. Except I am in control. I have a safe place to process and even if it's the ugly cry for three hours, then it's the ugly cry for three hours. Better out than shoving them in.

We have become so numb to our emotions and when big ones come up we get scared and want to check-out. This is too much. Give me meds to get over it. But is it too much? And are the meds really helping you get over it? I'm not against meds, I think they're a tool. But tools need to used properly. You can't achieve everything in a wood shop with only a hammer.

One, rest was in order. I slept like I had never slept before, after I quit academia and moved. When your nervous system finally feels safe, you sleep.

Two, find a job. Do something that is somewhat in alignment with your values. This was an absolute must for me. Even if it's temporary I have to do something with meaning and purpose.

Three, hire a trainer to replace physical therapy. I was beginning to regress and just knew I would be led to the right person who would listen to me, not treat me like a victim, and push me in a healthy way.

Four, find practitioners who would help heal at the root and who actually listened to me.

I had to surrender at a deep level. I had to trust that I was being lead to make these choices. I don't always have the words for the vision I have for my life, but I do hold the vibration of it and I know how I want to feel. It's this act, the holding onto how I want to feel, that I call the ritual of the magician. And I keep showing up like the worker bee diligently working and trusting that God has me as I continue to hold this vision.

This is the real surrender. The part where you trust your instincts when everyone else is like WTF are you doing with your life?

IT TAKES A VILLAGE

People who take personal development seriously talk about perceived setbacks. When you feel like you're going backwards, but in fact you're still progressing forward in growth.

For about two years, the left side of my body was numb. The heel-tow action was practically nonexistent in the left foot giving me the appearance of a slight limp. And my legs felt heavy all the time.

I remember how elated I was when I got my normal walking pace back.

Working with a spinal specialist, taking supplements, doing somatic dance movement, and going to the gym to lift weights regularly have helped me improve at an insane rate. In January, 2023 I RAN on the treadmill for 10 seconds and I cried! I have been pushing every week seeing improvements cognitively, physically, and spiritually. Because I believe above all else that this is a spiritual journey. The physical healing is its own rollercoaster once you understand how to navigate the constant shifting of symptoms.

It's not always a steady incline of improvements, though. Sometimes, in the healing journey it FEELS like you become stagnant, or worse it FEELS like you're going backwards. Obviously, I'm not a neuroscientist, I'm a person dealing with ripple effects from a TBI and can only tell you what it has been like from my perspective.

In 2023, three years after the accident, I found myself over stimulated from birthday messages and how it exhausted my brain to the point where I needed help driving. Thank you to trusted friends who really held space for me that day! Thank you to myself for allowing myself to be seen that way and receive the much needed assistance. Healing a traumatic brain injury won't allow you to override your system no matter how hard you try to push through those symptoms. You absolutely have to stop and take care of it.

It's a gift if you think about it. It demands you be fully in the present moment and tend to your needs and learn to do it unapologetically.

When my mind or body are overstimulated, or when I push way beyond what it can handle, symptoms pop up without my ability to immediately get a handle on it. It requires my full attention. Calming the vagus nerve is the only way to calm this body. And then resting so my brain can recharge.

I actually don't show people this side of my recovery even though I talk openly about my healing journey. It can be overwhelming to witness and it's definitely overwhelming to go through. What does help, is putting ice on my wrists or chest and controlling my breath.

I go to a gym that has classes for lifting. Especially after the TBI, I feel safe lifting in these classes after building a safe connection with the coaches. The programming is really smart and I'm witnessing amazing growth in everyone! It can be a lot for a brain that hasn't been injured. You're seeing 8-14 people doing different or similar movements, you're hearing loud music, you're counting in your head, the lighting is bouncing off equipment, there's side conversations, you're trying to remember every move you just learned, you're telling your body to move your legs and your arms in opposite directions… the list continues. Try breaking down every element you're seeing, hearing, feeling in a busy workout class.

Now try to add in TBI symptoms: vertigo, dizziness, nausea, nerve pain, nerve tingling, numbness, certain muscles turning on and off in the middle of a move, your spatial awareness is altered, hearing is muffled, your speech is off, your brain turns your ability to read text and makes it look like a different language, counting is a challenge (what are numbers?), motor functions are off, just to name a few. No seriously, I have lost track of some of the symptoms I was going through.

I show up exactly as I am and do each movement to the best of my ability. I give 100% of wherever I am on that given day. Each day is different, and I know that each hour within the day is different.

I'm beyond grateful I'm out of the majority of these symptoms. And for the most part I'm operating from a place of almost normal and I hear all the time, "I would not know you have suffered a TBI." Sometimes a flare up can confuse me but healing this isn't like healing a sprained wrist. There's no time limit and there's no one particular symptom that flares up. Sometimes, I have found myself in deep gratitude and frustration simultaneously.

It's like all the 2x4s before the accident were sharpening my tools prepping me for the long haul of healing the TBI. It's like I was exercising a muscle of trusting and surrendering. So, when the accident did happen, I was able to let go on a level I hadn't experienced before. There was also no way of escaping this. No movie, song, or activity could allow me to escape or soothe the discomfort. I had no other choice but to navigate the bizarre experience of this.

A little over a year into the TBI, I enrolled in a friend's group course. She was teaching somatic dance movement and something within me grabbed my attention every time I saw a post or video from her.

I could barely move. All I could do was move my arms, stand up and sit down almost right away. Dancing, is not what I would call it. With her method, I began to improve drastically and my physical therapist was thrilled. I started to develop my own techniques and methods from what I was learning from her. I was committed and took all three of her group courses.

The feminine is not meant to do it alone. My friend says, "We're meant to lone wolf it together." She's right. No one can come in and save you, only you can do that and you don't have to do it alone or without support.

Before enrolling in her third and final course, I tried to quit. Something in me could sense BIG change coming and my ego wanted to bail. "There is power in being witnessed." This is what I heard right before the course started. So, I enrolled, and yes, big change happened. Allowing myself to be seen by these women was powerful for both of us. And them allowing me to witness their growth was powerful for both of us. Some of them witnessed my growth in all three courses and their feedback reflected great transformation.

When you're in it, really working hard to improve, you don't realize where you started. And by the end of the third course I was moving and my body was expressing in a way that I never thought was possible. Even before the accident.

Own exactly who you are while pushing for growth and your community will naturally form. Because it's when we find ourselves within community that we are at our strongest. This is a sacred act of connection.

CREATION AFTER RISING FROM THE ASHES

Having had so many blatant messages hit me over and over again, and having the ability of taking complex information, filtering it, and then presenting it in bite sized chunks to others; I've allowed myself to follow a new creative path.

Remember that vision I had on the couch in New Jersey? I didn't know it at the time but that vision was the frequency of a vow to create a safe space for women.

I've been teaching women empowerment and how to create safety both with and for their bodies. Having had so many experiences where my personal safety and my body have been compromised, I've decided to teach women how to create it for themselves. Because that's ultimately what I've been doing for myself.

Listening to your inner whisper or intuition is a sacred connection. It's a space when you quiet the mind and surrender that you notice you're being nudged in a certain direction. It might be uncomfortable and it might scare you at first, but it's always inspiring. That's your higher soul requesting you turn to that direction.

Did you learn how to do this in school? Did you learn how to process your emotions in K-12? Did you learn how to listen to your inner knowing? If you answered no, my next question is did your parents help teach you how to do this? If you answered no again, there's a reason why my soul signed up to process big emotional scenarios and why I feel called to facilitate this.

The fact that I was sitting on a couch in New Jersey with my grandmother and mother when I had this vision are no accident. Breaking generational patterns is part of the process. I come from a long line of women who hold in their emotions AND who hold their breath. I can hear my grandmother's voice in my head as I type this, "I'm breathing, I'm still alive aren't I?!?" I love her fire! I always wanted to ask, "But do you FEEL alive?" That question would have been like speaking Japanese to her. How you're breathing contributes to your emotional well-being.

Quite frankly, I never really knew what joy felt like until I began to purge what I was holding onto and stretching the edge of what I knew. What that looks like is different for everyone. And I really didn't start to make much progress until I began to unlock the stagnant rhythm of breathing.

"Fake it til you make it." Have you heard of this saying? What if we shifted this phrase to fit the context of what we're talking about? (Breathing with intention of letting go of stuck emotions.) What if we shifted this phrase to, "Have the intention of releasing all stored anger, just breathe." If you show up consistently with this intention sooner or later a shift begins to happen. It might not be right away but with consistency change happens because energy follows intention.

I have a client who has felt disconnected from her body for years. I relate to her story because of my own healing. When she is in her body and connected she can be critical of what she's experiencing. She just went through my level 1 course and the change I see in her is remarkable! She moves with empowerment and her inner critic is now much more graceful. She feels gratitude for the movement she does have, though it may be limited for now, she's ecstatic for the growth she's accomplished.

Focusing on breath with movement has helped her alchemize her emotions. It's not always easy. In fact, when stored emotions come to the surface after years of being suppressed it can be uncomfortable. But now she has the tools to process these emotions more effectively. Because it's through body movement with the combination of our intention and breath that we are able to unlock emotions that have been stored in the body.

It takes an average of 18 days to create a new habit. What if you set the intention to release all stored anger with every single exhale of this breathing exercise?

And what if you don't feel angry? I don't *feel* angry, but I also know that there might be some of that emotion stored in my body. Did you just read my personal story? Who wouldn't be angry at all those boundaries being violated? Anger is an emotion showing us where boundaries need to be or where those boundaries were violated. Without judgment, I show up with intention to release what has been stored in the body.

What if grief is the major emotion you're hanging onto? Okay, have that intention of releasing that with every exhale. Make it work for you and where you are now. Give yourself a safe space to cry it out, yell it out in a pillow, hit your mattress… you get the idea.

A go to of mine is inhale for 6 seconds—hold for 3—exhale for 6 seconds—hold for 3. Repeat this at least three times. At the very least, you'll recognize that you're releasing something or feel more relaxed afterwards. Who doesn't like feeling relaxed?

The sacred feminine is nurturing *and* receiving. We dance in the creative process. Those of us that embody the sacred feminine (it doesn't matter what gender you are or what you identify with, I'm talking about frequency here), our intuition is attuned to the divine. A lot of us have been programmed by society and we have forgotten how to listen.

There's a lot of inner child work and meditative approaches that we dive into in my courses. I create a container to hold space as clients navigate deep shredding of their old patterns and egos. Having a client feel safe is my number one priority. I also hold space for sexual empowerment and remind you that you cannot step into your goddess energy until your inner child feels safe. There's so much out of balance that when you find equilibrium, this is your foundation to step forward as a confident individual.

Because of what I've been through and sought, system after system, and method after method, of healing deep rooted trauma, I have cultivated my own way of creating safety with and for you. I consider it to be a sacred act of co-creating a space and witness your growth.

"I choose me. I'm not an option, I'm *the* option." I don't consider myself a teacher for my clients. I'm a practitioner working alongside them creating a space with and for them to remember who they truly are. Helping them to remember that their power is in their choices. After so much rejection, I still choose to follow my dreams and I have no doubt that facilitating in this way is part of my purpose. Writing my story for you is part of my purpose and that purpose continues to grow and reveal itself to me.

For me, this is sacred connection. To leap forward not fully knowing with my logical mind but trusting that all is truly okay.

Much like the Phoenix dancing in the flames, I have found myself doing the same but in grace on fire. A fire that burns deep within me allowing myself to be reborn.

If Lindsay's story resonated with you and you'd like to get in touch, scan the QR code to schedule a free consultation, follow her on instagram, or receive helpful tips to embody inner peace by joining her newsletter.

https://linktr.ee/lindsayleelionheart

Michele Leeper

Michele speaks the language of love. She came into this world as a multi-dimensional old soul, with a huge compassion for humanity. She is a lighthouse for seekers who desire to cultivate their own inner sanctuary.

Michele's path includes working with women recovering from addiction and domestic violence. For over a decade, she facilitated support groups and volunteered as a first responder for women in crisis. Michele is a bestselling Author, Empowerment Coach, and Embodiment Guide.

3) SOLAR PLEXUS – EMBODIMENT

A WOMAN REBORN

by Michele Leeper

I loved myself as a child. I was a free-range kid full of curiosity, and I disliked wearing clothes as much as I disliked my German mother's liver and onions on Sundays! My family called me Mickey. I would spend my summer days at the creek, berry picking in the hills behind my grandparents' farmhouse, or somewhere up in the treetops. I enjoyed making mud pies and grass salads that I offered to the barn cats and my grandma's little dog, Checkers. As I got a little older, I played softball, practiced dance routines, and did gymnastics in the yard. My little girl self was full of joy and wonder. I'd say that I was going to be a famous movie star when I grew up. One of my favorite things to do was to dress up and put on shows for my family. I knew that I was adorable! Adults called me precocious.

Everything changed for me somewhere around eight years old. My parents divorced when I was three years old, and I lived with my mother. My mom had her own baggage and was constantly running from something. At that time, she had moved us to a small town in Iowa. I went to a new school and became good friends with a neighbor boy from church. I sang in the choir, was a girl scout, and had a paper route. I was a wholesome Midwest American girl… and I was so much more. I was also a budding flower, and because of that, there was a lot of conflict at home between my mother and me. I was curious and asked challenging questions that made people uncomfortable. I wanted to know about the story of Adam and Eve, how we all got here, and WHY we were all here, for example.

One day after church, our pastor asked me to help him get some hymn books out of the basement. I went downstairs with him enthusiastically. The room was dusty, full of boxes and books, and had one small window with short green curtains on the far wall. The Pastor sat down in a wooden armchair and beckoned me to come sit on his lap. It felt like going to sit on Santa's lap, so I went over to him and hopped up. He was asking me questions and giving me compliments. Suddenly his energy changed. His hands were shaky and clammy as he patted my knee and started rubbing up my leg. I froze and my mind started racing. Inside I felt like I was falling down a tunnel and searching for something to brace myself with. I became stiff and dead quiet when his hand made its way under my dress and over the top of my yellow flowered panties. I stared straight ahead at the window and noticed the specks of dust floating in a sunbeam. I felt that something very wrong was happening, but I couldn't move or speak. It was the first time I can remember leaving my body.

I don't know how long I was away from my body before a woman from the congregation knocked on the door. When she called his name, he pushed me off and gave me a strange look before quickly opening the door. I walked out of that horrible room and looked straight through the woman standing there. I said nothing to anyone the rest of the day. This is my earliest memory of experiencing shame. It was the calm before the storm… when all the birds stop singing.

I told my mom about what had happened at the church, and she slapped me across the face so hard that I cut my lip on my teeth and drew blood. She told me to shut my filthy demon mouth! In her blinding anger she decided to cut all my long hair off that night to punish me. I had loved her unconditionally until that very moment when I realized that she wasn't going to protect me. It seemed to me at the time that saving her "reputation" was more important to her. She was lost, stumbling through the valley of her shadow since her own childhood. I felt like a blemish on her white Christian robe. I was her mirror, reflecting things about her own painful abuse that she couldn't free herself from. I didn't trust her after that. I felt abandoned, alone, and terrified by the darkness I felt eclipsing my broken heart. I stood looking at my reflection in the bathroom mirror crying and wondering who or what this had made me into. I reached into my pocket and pulled out a tube of cherry red lip-gloss that I'd stolen from the store earlier that morning, and I applied it carefully pausing to look into my hurt little ocean blue-green eyes. Then, I angrily smeared it all over my face and cried myself to sleep on the cold bathroom floor.

I spent years believing that there was something wrong with me and that I was a "bad seed." The most heartbreaking part of it was that I believed that I must have done something to deserve it. In those early years, I was raised to believe that women of virtue didn't ask questions or speak unless spoken to, and that children were meant to be seen and not heard. This is the origin of my mother wound that festered and grew like a cancer inside my cells for years.

The messages we receive as children become our beliefs about ourselves and our reality. These are the toxic frequencies that get stuck in our bodies and cause diseases. Releasing the not-so-happy memories and emotions associated with them is the inner child work we get to do to begin healing. Next comes our inner teenager, and chances are she's angry! Most of my sacred rage lived in my hips and belly and I started suffering painful cramping and digestive issues.

When was the first time you can remember being silenced or made to feel shame? Can you identify where in your body these feelings may be trapped, now?

FORGED IN FIRE

I have a vivid memory of my sixteen-year-old self, curled up naked in a claw foot bathtub, with the shower running over me. The room was filled with steam as I let all the hot water run cold. My body felt vacant and numb, and I held the soft flesh of my belly in my hands. I looked with a blank face, as blood mixed with water and made its way across the porcelain and down the drain. I don't exactly recall when I had become a "cutter". It was what I did to try to feel something... anything other than how I felt, which was frozen. I didn't want to be in a female body. It was complicated, uncomfortable, and I loathed it. I felt trapped within the layers of fat, muscles, and bones of it. I often wondered if I could cut my breasts off, sew myself back together and not die from some awful infection, or make myself more hideous than I already felt. By then, I had endured incredible violence, including sexual and domestic abuse—often from those that were supposed to protect me, and other times by people having a position of authority. I often wondered if I gave off a "damaged goods" scent, because my energy seemed to attract predators. I held rage so fierce inside me that I feared hurting others. I instead took my anger out on myself. I often thought that I would burn the world down if I let myself feel it all, so I numbed to escape, tried to commit suicide several times, and was hospitalized with complex post-traumatic stress disorder (CPTSD).

At that time, the doctors, and those in charge of my welfare, had me taking a pharmacy cocktail of Prozac, Lithium, and Trazodone, for "manic-depression" and anxiety. I floated through my days feeling like trauma on bones and that my soul had been scooped out of me. I had put forty extra pounds on my petite five-foot-two frame, as a side effect from all the medications I was taking. I was living in a foster home (not my first or last) with a childless couple who favored fast food. I ate whatever they ate and then would make myself throw it up afterwards. I didn't have great guidance around healthy eating habits and, much like getting drunk or high, food became an addiction. Bulimia, an eating disorder of extreme binging and purging, gave me a morbid sense of control and safety.

Self-masochism and addiction were how I dealt with my disassociation from unprocessed trauma, and everything else in my life, at that time. I have great compassion and deep forgiveness for my younger self. I didn't understand how to regulate my nervous system and I did what I felt I had to for survival. I wear my scars like laugh lines, or map lines of the roads I've traveled.

There are so many reasons for leaving our body. Simply reading this now could bring up an uncomfortable body response. Should that be the case, I invite you to stand up and allow your body to move the way it wants to... stretch, sway, shake it out, take some centering breaths through your nose, release it with a sigh, and drink some water. Pay attention to any discomfort, pain, stress, fatigue, or resistance that presents itself as you navigate reading the rest of this. If you choose, journal anything that comes up. See if you can identify where the discomfort is in your body and name the emotion that is stored there. Your body is processing energy right now, so tune into its brilliant wisdom.

EXPLORING THE WRECK

For many years, I was angry with the God of my understanding and couldn't fathom why such terrible things could happen in this world. I did not want to identify as a victim, yet I wanted to be rescued. I wanted to be safe, loved, and accepted. I wanted to be someone worthy of loving. I wanted to be a wife and a mother. I wanted to belong, so I became a shapeshifter. I learned to be who other people wanted me to be, and in the process became even more disconnected from my body and spirit. I was acting, trying on different masks, costumes, and characters. The messages I received from the world were that I wasn't enough, that I was broken, and sometimes that I was too much. I didn't know how to be in my own skin, so, I was continuously looking for validation from outside of myself. I went from person to person, relationship after relationship, and then to some very dark places when I felt rejected. Like a serpent eating its own tail, I was spinning out of control in my vicious cycle. I felt like an insatiable black hole, and I didn't know how to fill the void.

In my early twenties, I got pregnant with my first child. My entire pregnancy, for a variety of reasons, felt like an invasion of a body snatcher. My womb was a hostile war zone... instead of the beautiful center of creation and bridge between the heavens and earth it is intended to be. I felt like a toxic wasteland, and I simply could not embrace sharing my body with the life growing inside it. As a result, my first son was born with many abnormalities and challenges. Soon into my third trimester, my body completely stopped being viable enough to nourish his growth to completion. At first, this seemed to be evidence (to me) that there was in fact something "wrong" with me. However, something primal and deeply instinctual was activated from within my spirit and being through that experience. Nonetheless, I physically struggled through both of my "high risk" pregnancies. Before becoming pregnant with my second son, I had been diagnosed with Type 1 diabetes and became insulin dependent. This felt like an insult to injury, but now the check engine light was on, so to speak. I had to pay attention to my body because the alternative was death! So, becoming a mother, and receiving a life-threatening diagnosis were the catalysts of my healing journey.

It took me most of my adult life to change my relationship with myself and my body. I wanted to be as free, joyful, and uninhibited as I remembered myself as a child. I could feel that my innocence was still alive within me, and that my inner child longed for connection, love, and safety. This was reflected to me through witnessing the joy and wonderment of my own children. I started to become more curious about the internal dialogue I'd been carrying around with me for so many years. Whose voice was I listening to? Where was all the blame, judgment and criticism coming from? I couldn't even imagine speaking that way to my children! How could I learn to parent my wounded inner child in the way that she needed, with encouragement, acceptance, and compassion? As an adult I was still punishing myself with self-rejection, self-harming, and pretending to be someone I wasn't to fit in, out of fear of further harm, humiliation, or punishment. I often felt like I was in prison, mind, body, and spirit, until I woke one day to realize that I had become the jailor. If I was the jailor, could I also be my liberator?

I could see too where my intimacy and full presence were limited in my parenting and with my partner, because of my mind/body disconnect. It took me another ten years after navigating an ugly divorce to truly realize that I AM RESPONSIBLE, for everything in my life—especially my own healing. I was broken open by the disappointment and heartache of ending my marriage, and it gifted me a metaphorical death to become a woman reborn. There is a lesson in everything if we are open to it. I was being invited into my own power! I came to learn how to use my inner fire to create, not destroy, through what felt like the biggest betrayal and rejection of my adult life. I violated the sanctity of that union in many ways, and mostly I betrayed myself by trying to change into someone I wasn't to be loved. To walk in this life with an open heart takes immense courage when there are enormous wounds around trust. Learning to trust ourselves after self-abandonment and trauma is a daily practice. I found that what I most desired was to be in a sacred connection with myself—all of me, so that I could therefore be in a sacred connection with all the people in my life, as well as those yet to come. I honor that we are all spirits having a human experience here in Earth school.

Furthermore, there is no need for comparison when it comes to trauma. We are not competing for the "Who had the shittiest life award"—if there were such a thing. And we do not pity those who have suffered things that we have not experienced. Pity is not compassion; it is judgment and disrespect. Self-pity is disrespecting ourselves as well. Not everyone grows up with emotional neglect, abuse, and abandonment issues, and you are not alone if you have. Some of you may have grown up with very loving parents and caregivers. However, all of us inherited our own anxieties, fears, and sometimes feelings of unworthiness from somewhere. Healing is a level playing field, welcome to anyone willing to step up. Being disconnected from our bodies cuts us off from our truth, our innate source of wisdom. When we listen to our bodies, we know how to release stored emotions instinctively. Has anyone ever asked you "What does your gut say?" And are you aware that we have more serotonin in our stomachs than in our brains? In the article, Serotonin & The Gut: The Gut-Brain Axis, Amy Myers, MD wrote, "Your body communicates in ways you aren't even aware of. In fact, your brain and your gut talk to each other all the time through hormones and neurotransmitters. This is known as the gut-brain axis. This communication system between your brain and your gut is a biochemical and physical network. That gut feeling you get or the butterflies in your stomach… that's real! It's actually your brain and gut talking to each other." She goes on to explain, "Your central nervous system consists of your brain and your spinal cord. It controls your thoughts and emotions, along with your breathing, heart rate, body temperature, and the release of some hormones. Your enteric nervous system, also known as 'second brain,' consists of 200-600 million neurons that move through your digestive system." This is important because regulating our nervous system is a part of self-soothing in embodiment work. And serotonin is the super happy hormone, the mood and sleep regulator.

THE RETURN HOME

Divine Discontent came howling in the night, knocking on my windows, and rattling me from my slumber. I recognized her voice as my own saying it was time to wake up from my forty year-long nightmare of self-rejection and return home to my body—to love and respect it as a holy temple.

We've all heard the stories and watched the movies about female archetypes becoming "the wicked witch" villain or the superhero. The truth is that we are all a little bit of both at some time or another. True healing is about integrating all parts of ourselves. We're not denying our shadow self in favor of the more "acceptable" sunnier, higher vibe parts of ourselves. We get to create a different relationship with our darker side and give those aspects of ourselves a healthier way to self-express. Life is a series of choices.

I made the decision to be my own hero and save myself. As Tony Robins says, "There is no fucking guru!" We each have our own golden key to unlock the cage.

I sought my own healing journey and evolution by exploring different things, and I will say that healing is not a linear process. I delved into my personal and spiritual ascension by exploring recovery programs, therapy, hypnosis, religion, spirituality, rituals, cleanses, and fasting, energy healing, shadow work, shamanism, chakra healing, performance arts, art therapy, sound healing, vision boards, coaching, workshops, leadership training, and finally somatic dance embodiment.

My deepest and most profound healing began when I discovered Somatic Dance Embodiment. It's a natural and powerful way for the body to detoxify, release, let go and heal from unprocessed emotions and trauma. I have a high propensity for answering the call to voyage into the unfamiliar. I trained as a Method actor for more than eight years and continued to have a disconnection with my body. I felt my passion stirring to say, hell YES, to something I knew nothing about then. In a round-a-bout way, I hid myself by spending most of my time living in my mind, ego, and intellect. So, I offer my personal experience and awakening which resulted from me choosing to trust this process.

My mission is to understand my experiences, integrate them, and use them to fuel me to become an even better version of myself. My desire is to continue to cultivate sacred connection with my Divine self and to be a lighthouse for others seeking the path. We are here to remember that we're all having a physical human experience, and we are all connected through our humanity and beyond. We weave our memories and emotions together and connect the dots of all our parts that were lost, separated, and undiscovered. We go into the darkness, down into the roots, to excavate the minerals of our experiences, because that is where we are made diamonds! A dear friend and colleague of mine says you must go to the roots to rise.

Our bodies remember everything in their DNA, and every human body has a story. We are made mostly of water—which has scientifically been proven to have memory. Biophysicist William Brown, wrote in an article for Resonance Science Foundation, "This has been compared to the human body, of which each is incredibly unique and has an individual DNA unlike any other. Whilst the human body is made up of 70% water, conclusions could be drawn from these new discoveries that human tears can hold a unique memory of an individual being, through the body's store of water hosting a complete store of information that is linked to individual experience. Suggesting that everyone is globally connected by the water in the human body which travels through ongoing journeys, whereby information along the way is always stored.".

Some of what we carry in our cellular memory is passed down from our ancestors. In my healing journey I came to realize that I carried within me some of my mother's trauma, my grandmother's, and great grandmother's... and on and on. History repeats itself until someone breaks the pattern. The privilege and gift to heal wasn't necessarily available then in the way it is today. I hope that through my healing journey that I contribute to the healing of my family lineage and to be a source of transformation in the world as well.

Through embodiment, we go into ourselves to release the energy that keeps us frozen and stuck. Through the process, it is possible to cultivate forgiveness, deep self-love, freedom, and confidence, thereby being able to connect with joy and pleasure whenever we choose to. Embodiment is a self-administered technique that invites you into the practice of conscious breathing, calming the mind, connecting with your body and energy, healing old trauma, and releasing from the pain body through free flow movement. It is possible to tap into our body's wisdom in a way that empowers us and roots us into conscious connection with self. We begin to create new energetic pathways in our body which expands our capacity to express ourselves with full emotionality. For thousands of years, Shamans and healers have used ecstatic dance enhanced by the frequencies of music or drumming, to be in connection and commune with the Divine source and to acquire information and guidance.

Whenever I do this, I feel my heart open, my chakras align, my kundalini rise, and my creative self-expression activated. I'm connected to the earth and grounded in my being. I'm connected to my higher self, my intuition and Divine source. I am connected to my passion and purpose. It all begins with breathing with attention as it brings us consciously into our bodies. We are coming back to life and beginning to trust being in our bodies again!

Stop right now and just try it! Close your eyes and take a slow, deep breath through your nose and then, slowly, let it out through your nose. Repeat this twice more. Doesn't that feel refreshing?

At first, you may feel a little resistant about trying this practice. Some of our conditioning as women has taught us that it's arrogant or it's not polite to be seen and take up too much space. Receive this now... You get to be seen, heard, and take up all the space you need!

I have received some feedback from others, who had watched videos that I posted, saying that they couldn't watch the entire thing. They said it was because it made them judge themselves for not being brave enough to do something like that, or that they've never imagined themselves wanting to do something such as this. I honor it if it's not something that is aligned for you. Own it. Take what you need from this and leave the rest. It's a sovereign decision. But don't let fear keep you small! You will thank yourself later. Furthermore, it doesn't require any special skills or fancy dance moves to practice embodiment. Your body will tell you how it wants to move when it's ready. It's about setting an intention and then creating a safe container to let our inner child out to play. Making my Inner child feel welcome and safe is where I started my journey. When I began this work as a participant, I sat holding my heart, hugging myself, swaying side to side and crying, my first class. That's what I needed in that moment to release my inner resistance. My mantra is: "I allow myself to be exactly as I am at this moment."

This is a healing journey that I now guide others through. I have shared some of my stories; the source of my pain and dis-ease, how it has shown up in my relationship with myself and others, as well as the results that were created within me. If you feel called to explore healing through somatic dance embodiment, then I encourage you to step into that commitment to yourself now... Because LIFE IS NOW! Join me for a FREE discovery call to discuss how I can support you in expanding your healing journey and your vision for your life. To schedule, check out my website:

www.micheleleeper.com

As we return to our own essence and become our own sanctuary, we remember that we are Divine, and we are powerful creators. We get to manifest our dreams and desires with pleasure and limitless possibilities from that sacred place of knowing within. We are the magnificent treasures that prevail!

Dr. Jennifer Markham, ND

Dr. Jennifer Markham, is a visionary artist, naturopathic doctor, teacher, writer, and speaker. She supports individuals in reversing chronic disease with quantum healing therapeutics. She educates, inspires, and empowers individuals to harmonize their body, mind, and spirit. True healing is a journey from dissonance/dis-ease to resonance with one's true soul Self. She is passionate in bringing together communities for healing, education, creative arts, food, dance, play, and experiences, which support living in harmony with nature.

4) HEART – VIBRATION

BE IN TUNE

by Dr. Jennifer Markham, ND

"If you want to find the secrets of the universe, think in terms of energy, frequency and vibration."
—NIKOLA TESLA

When Ann asked me to be part of *Sacred Connection*, I said yes, and later when she asked if I would like to contribute in this book, I said to let me feel into it and check back in with me, as I had a lot of changes happening in my life and wondered, would I be able to commit and fulfill this opportunity? Ultimately, I said yes, which is obvious, yet the way in which my theme was chosen is a story within itself. Over the past nearly three years, I have had the privilege of knowing Ann, and interacting on a daily basis for well over a year in a sacred container, so when I say we did not find the time to talk about the book for months, you might be wondering how that was possible.

We weren't avoiding one another, we were sharing meaningful conversations daily! One day, I said to go ahead and give me a call, let's talk about the book, and she intended to do just that, but then something came up and she ended up having a conversation with Alicia Power which turned into *her* becoming a co-author of this beautiful collaborative piece. The day Ann and I got on the phone, the theme we had been dancing around for me was indeed fit for another, and I wondered if maybe our timing with this conversation had missed its moment. We kept at the conversation, exploring the various themes that already weave through my world as an explorer of the sacred. Numerology, music, healing, and nature. Then Ann offered, vibration, and my heart jumped in my chest, my body tingled a little, and I smiled. "I resonate with vibration," I said.

You see, years ago I studied music therapy, having been a pianist since the age of three. I was accepted into the program through my piano audition, and although I did not continue studying that major, my passion for music and sound as therapy only continued. Since my youth, music, sound, harmonics, frequency, and quantum healing modalities have all enriched my life. As a naturopathic doctor in private practice for seven years now, I continue to incorporate and deepen my understanding and experience of vibrational healing modalities, and their amazing effects on reversing dis-ease. Since my youth, I remained passionate in the understanding that not only song, but most simplistically, frequency and harmonics, are the most profound waves in which our cells respond. Therefore, our organs function, and our entire being exists in harmony or disharmony. Whoa, Ann! We "found" it! We found the theme that has been passionately woven throughout my entire life, spending hours playing music and singing, learning to create overtones with my own voice, and teaching others while reminding whoever is listening, that everything is frequency, everything is vibration, every thing is energy.

Within normal childhood development, when a child's permanent teeth begin coming in, typically around the age of six, the brain wave activity switches from **theta** brain waves (4-7 Hertz) to **alpha** brain waves (8-13Hz). Meaning, a child goes from a deep meditative, dreaming, half-awake type stage of life between ages two and six, into a visualizing, meditative, hypnotic trance of sorts, downloading beliefs related to self, state. Between ages six and nine, I became aware of my focus on spirit, God, and truth. Perceivable before that age, as children are, I was observing my environment, dreaming, learning what to believe, and witnessing the suffering and joy of others around me. So, from youth, I was interested in matters of the soul and spirit, spending days alone in nature or with the animals, meditating, listening, and being. It is no wonder that I intuitively understood vibration and frequency, such that thoughts create reality or at the least alter reality. When a baby is played certain types of music in utero, there have been studies which showed those babies, as they grew and developed, had greater cognitive development, increased intelligence, and increased creativity. Music which evokes positive emotions or is soothing to us can support a positive immune response, positive mood and emotional response.

During my undergraduate years, while studying music therapy, I took a physics course, for fun. That's right. I really wanted to know about quantum physics, but I needed to start somewhere, as college goes. It turns out that my very cool professor understood the unique lens through which I viewed life, and perhaps he knew that I was only going to make it through his class if he delved into the world of quantum, so he did. Or perhaps he already found quantum reality unavoidable. Either case, bless him! Before I share more about that physics class, there is one very profound memory that has returned to my conscious mind many times over the years, from fourth grade. I was sitting in class, a science class, I presume. The teacher was talking about molecules, atoms, electrons, protons, and forces. Whether he said it or I thought it, I remember my mind metaphorically exploding with a realization. Everything is energy, frequency and vibration, and minute matter or then, objects, appear as real because we exist within a particular environment. We believe the table to exist because it holds paper and a pencil, but everything that makes up the table is in constant motion. Objects are mostly made of free space, according to the way we were taught about atoms. Therefore if forces, such as gravity, stay consistent, which they are not always, then objects appear as real and remain "held together" to our observation. While that may not seem so mind-bending to an adult, when that information reached my consciousness at nine-years-old, my curiosity about what is indeed real and true about our perceived environment was greatly peaked. Everything is changeable under the right conditions, and everything is effectively always in motion, vibrating, affected by other frequencies, and this thrilled me. It wasn't until years later, in organic chemistry, when I learned of the studies of *quantum non-locality* done by Nicolas Gisin, a Swiss physicist and professor, that my knowing was bolstered yet again.

It was the results of these studies which enlivened my intuition and sense of true reality. An experiment was done; indeed several reproducible experiments were done. There were photons, split into pairs of photons traveling apart to two different locations in Switzerland, 10km apart on fiber-optic cables, where they each met their detector. The photons' responses were observed and measured in their respective detectors. The detectors allowed the researchers to assess the response and activity of the photon, or quantum particle, carrier of electromagnetism. What I recall from the experiment was that when the researcher made the decision to do something to the one photon, the very instant he did that thing to one photon, the other photon, the one nearly seven miles away, responded as though that same thing had just been done to it. Instantaneous equal response due to the quantum nature and Oneness of all.

Explained another way, someone in Bellevue tossed a coin, and when they grabbed it out of midair it was heads up, and every time this happened, simultaneously in Bernex, seven miles away, another person observed their coin go from spinning to stopping heads up, at the exact same moment, every time. This photon experiment was reproduced, and thus, the heads up coin was seen thousands of times. What this confirmed for me was that factors, such as time and space, are not true factors after all. That, in fact, limitations which appear to be real based on distance or time, are perhaps much more related to one's belief. Or was the size of the matter observed a true limitation? After all, photons are quantum particles. What about something the size of a car? How far apart in the world can you be from another human being, and yet feel when they are about to call or text you? Is that not accessing information from a greater, unseen field, a field of consciousness, or rather the subconscious field? These researchers observed simultaneous equal responses which occurred over and over. Was this because the photons were relatively close? Further experiments were done with the photons about 60km apart with the same results.

When we observe something, with intention, is that not having an effect on the thing(s) we are observing too? I enjoy considering and understanding life at this quantum level, because it coincides with my spiritual and natural experiences. While schooling tends to teach reductionism, the breaking apart of the whole and fixating on one area, as is done in most "scientific studies," I have found in life, and in practice, much greater results in understanding and supporting the whole of a being, by looking at the whole of the being. Imagine that! So, how does a thought not affect reality, if stress can alter the effects of the immune response or clarity of thought, and we understand this? Of course, it does all come down to what you believe.

Those experiments prompted for me that thought, intention alone has a profound effect on particles which are not in the same location, not even close by, and without any delay in time whatsoever. This brings me full circle back to sitting in fourth grade, realizing that everything exists due to minute (quantum particles), vibrations, forces, and beliefs. Years later, it was affirmed for me that thoughts and intentions are so powerful and that time and space do not limit their reach or effects. Life has simply become more magical, each moment a glorious opportunity to observe the said mysteries of the universe. My experience tells me that we are a microcosm of the macrocosm, therefore, we are the universe, and a lifetime of searching for meaning or answers can be distilled down to the truth is within us. We are spiritual beings having a human experience. This was a discovery which came to me spontaneously as an adult during a deeply profound healing and awakening period. Years later, I discovered many other beings have said something very similar, although I had never read that myself or followed a particular guru, per se. Which leads me to, the truth is the truth, and is recognized because it is universally so. We feel perhaps like an "ah ha," or an excited or peaceful recognition. We know. It is not a statement of, I think therefore I am, but I Am that I Am.

As Don Miguel Ruiz states in The Fifth Agreement, "It's something that you just know; it's something that you can feel without words, and it's called *silent knowledge*. Silent knowledge is what you know before you invest your faith in symbols. When you open yourself to the truth, and learn to listen, then all the symbols lose their value, and the only thing that remains is the truth. There's nothing to know; there's nothing to justify." Let the pure light and truth within you, before knowledge came to teach you what to believe and what was "true," guide your way *home*.

A family friend introduced us to a quantum healing modality when I was 18-years old. This machine and program knew what traumas had occurred in my life, at what age, and what organ systems and emotions were inhibiting my body, mind, and spirit from being in harmony, as related to past experiences. The machine, created by the main space agency of the United States, known as NASA, was banned from medical use in this country because it can heal individuals from such things as cancer. If this is the first time you have encountered the concept that the medical system is not a health-care system, I will simply leave it to say here, the medical system in the developing world, is a sick care system. Of course, there are kind hearted, people with positive intentions who are physicians, trying to provide good quality care to many, and who are themselves frustrated by a system built on drugs and surgeries, but the history to their entire system is an easily accessible read, and just a little observation and common sense can show that for being a country with the greatest expenses in healthcare, we have one of the sickest populations. You aren't having a headache because you are deficient in acetaminophen. Let's just say that! And, in my experience, you don't have to just live with it! Educating, inspiring, and empowering individuals on their healing journey—a journey to wholeness is one of my greatest passions. That machine is not necessary to reverse disease, but it taught me many things.

One incredible piece of knowledge that came from my experience with this device, was that healing occurs, ultimately, and simply, at the vibrational or quantum level. This machine, and others which I have had the privilege of working with over the years, could potentize water, or make in essence a homeopathic remedy, to become a vibratory healing elixir. One could simply say, the water contained an equal vibrational frequency of the dis-ease in the body, for which, when drank, supported the whole body to return to balance. This is easily explained by another physics experiment.

I walked into the physics classroom, noticing that particular day was likely about frequencies or waves. There were two speakers setup on either side of the room, both facing slightly inward toward our seats. What the professor proceeded to demonstrate with the two speakers helps explain the common homeopathic concept expressing the law of similars, "like cures like." Homeopathy is a system in medicine, which uses remedies to assist the return to health and harmony. A homeopathic remedy is a diluted substance, in essence a vibrational substance, typically void of any physical substance at all, but rather an energetic signature of the intended thing, in a substrate, like water. A homeopathic remedy, when prescribed appropriately, can have a profound effect on the physical, emotional, mental, and spiritual body, respectfully. For example, the homeopathic remedy Coffee cruda, may be a great remedy for someone experiencing jitteriness, diaphoresis, rapid speech, rapid loose stools, or other classic coffee ingester symptoms. Or Aconite, known as a quick-acting poison, when used homeopathically, may be useful in the case of anaphylaxis when there is a feeling that death is impending, sudden onset of high fever, flushing of the skin, restlessness, anxiety, terror, etc. "Like cures like" because of the similitude, the equal frequencies of the remedy and the symptoms cancel out, leaving the desired effects, the symptoms cease. Our professor began by playing some sound waves, frequencies from each speaker, one at a time, and so initially we heard the sounds. Then, he had the speakers turned to face one another, and the sounds ceased to exist, no sound was heard. The frequencies matched and canceled out in the air, or almost completely canceled out. The frequencies existed, although not seen by the naked eye, and when the sound waves met in "mid-air" there was nowhere for them to go, the waves became null. This was due to the way the speakers were set up, so that the sound waves were equal yet out-of-phase, inverted. In the case of the body and homeopathic, or dilute vibrational substances, like cures like because when the dissonance of the dis-ease process in the body is matched by the equal vibrational resonance of the remedy, they cancel out, and the perceived and experienced symptoms cease. So, back to the machine which potentized water to my body's needs. I was fascinated by the knowledge that water could contain a message to heal. This deepened my fascination with quantum healing.

In 2001, the internationally renowned Japanese scientist, Masaru Emoto wrote a book, *The Hidden Messages in Water*. Using a high-speed camera, he successfully photographed water as it formed crystalline structures, i.e. snowflakes. He photographed pure spring water, polluted and toxic water, water exposed to beautiful harmonious music, screeching metal music, written words of negativity, demands, hatred, joy, and love. If you are unfamiliar, you can imagine what the snowflakes revealed. Loving words, positive intentions, pure water, and beautiful music, all created glorious, colorful, symmetrical, perfect, intricate, and unique snowflakes. Whereas, hateful, negative words, disharmonious sounds, and polluted waters created asymmetrical, distorted or warped shapes, even lacking a true snowflake structure. The book, full of beautiful colorful photographs, quickly affirmed what is simply felt internally by listening to peaceful music versus chaotic sounds. By drinking pure water versus polluted water. By speaking words of love and truth to one's self and others, versus lies, fear, and hatred.

There are two things I further want to share with you in regards to the messages in water. One, Dr. Emoto was not initially successful in his first two months of attempting to capture images of the frozen water and create consistent, repeatable results capable of being documented. He found out later that shortly after he was successful, other researchers were then successful in doing the same thing. Emoto, due to his success with water, ended up having conversations with a Dr. Rupert Sheldrake, a researcher and professor, essentially interested in the unseen. Sheldrake described this phenomena as *morphic resonance*. For example, when things are claimed to be impossible, never having occurred before, until one day that thing happens, and then it happens again and again. A resonance, intention, shift, change in focus, change in conditions, change in beliefs, something has allowed the change to occur, and once it happens once, morphic resonance explains why it happens again and from thence forth.

Emoto and other researchers were all putting their energy and attention toward successfully creating the conditions for their individual experiments to be viable and viewable, and once he was successful, then without sharing how he was successful, the other researchers became successful. Another example is, at one time it was believed that no one could run faster than a 4-minute mile, until someone did, and then several others have. This I share, because this brings up another aspect of vibration and the quantum world, one of intention and resonance. When two or more individuals put their intention and energy toward something, they bring about the potentiality of it occurring, based on belief, which affects the quantum, invisible world, all the way up to the physical world. I have heard that once an idea is born, stated, and intended, whether the individual who spoke it or not becomes the creator, the intention has been born in the field, and the invention becomes created somehow, someway, by someone accessing the thought in the *mind field*.

The powerful effect of morphic resonance may be just as possible when many are focusing on false evidence appearing as real, or fear. For example, millions of people are watching television, listening to mainstream news, who are all owned by the same 5-6 mega corporations, which tell you the "truth" they want you to know about happenings in the world; the sick, twisted, violent, terrible, scary, disgusting, pointless, and hopeless nature of it all. These millions of people are focusing their attention on what they are told to focus their attention on, mindlessly programmed, often quite sure they must know what's going on to be a proper citizen, a good aware human, and the right kind of person. Consider for a moment, if you will, if the energy of three people focusing on the exciting possibility of a new experiment becoming possible caused the quantum field to shift making it actually possible in the physical world, how much more powerful millions of individuals can create and perpetuate reality, based on thinking about, believing, and talking about the narrative of fear, violence, distrust, unrest, illness, pestilence, lies, and disease. Put another way, life is not what you believe it to be, it is exactly what you believe it to be. What do you believe then? It is most definitely a choice, although initially the subconscious is programmed before the age of six, in what to believe and what is said, "truth." This can be undone and cleared, through awareness, yes, but in my experience, through the desire for Truth. I love supporting and witnessing individuals experience revelations of truth and freedom within themselves. Someone very wise and whole was to have said, "The Truth shall set you Free." And, so it does.

The second thing I wanted to share concerning the hidden messages in water is the inevitability of the oppositional viewpoint. For example, I can think of a few dear friends who love to listen to screaming heavy metal music. They may not say that this type of music induces relaxation, yet they do specifically enjoy the loud chaotic screaming sounds over other types of music. This reminds me of when individuals feel most at home when there is constant noise of some type, such as the television, radio, or fans blowing. In my medical observation, this is due to a programmed response of the nervous system. Meaning, an internal chaotic environment, a representation of the activity or balance of one's autonomic nervous system, can feel more soothed by an external chaotic stimulus, because it is similar, familiar. Remember like cures like. The sympathetic nervous system, the one responsible for running away from the lion, once stimulated, if it does not deem the physical body or emotional body to be in a safe environment, i.e. without disease or emotionally nurtured, it will continue to run about ruling the roost, in your defense. An imbalanced autonomic nervous system, or stimulated sympathetic system is, in part, why we have a love for speed, fast cars, loud fast-paced movies, stimulants, adrenaline rushes, spicy foods, excessive exercise, constant talking, poor sleep, tension, and so on. Imagine a car at the top of a hill, rolling down now, there is one foot certainly on the gas, and depending on how long your body or you have been on the run and how many reserves or how much fuel you really have left in the tank, the other foot may also be on the brake. Run away, or provide stimulation now because something disastrous might happen. Also, I am exhausted, I can't go on like this for much longer, something has to give, and the parts on the car are giving up and giving out.

So, looking back at morphic resonance as it relates to negative or fear-driven intentions or focus, can negative words, thoughts, actions, intentions, chaotic violent sounds and noises really create balance and harmony? The more interesting question may be, what do you feel for you, yourself? Do you relax or find focus when hearing Mozart, Bach or other classical music? Or do you find the sound of soft rainfall or a babbling brook annoying? I have observed in countless individuals, including myself, that our preferences for sound, let alone just about everything, changes in time, especially during an intentional healing journey, the journey back to the True Self.

Life is a song, it goes on forever

Love is a dance that we do in the city, yeah

When you hear the sound of the whole world spinnin 'round

Listen to the rhythm of the river steady flowing out

Moving to it's own vibration

Singing harmonies with all of creation

We all play a part, yeah we all got a place

And love is infinite

Everything is Music

Everything is music, yeah

Everything is music, music

Everything is music

A beautiful song by Tubby (Andrew) Love, called *Everything Is Music*, portrays this lovely image to my heart and soul. I know I came to sing, play, and dance. I share this because perhaps you will become blissful while you listen to this song, because that's how music can be. It can and does move our heart and spirit. I share this song, because, everything is music, and everyone is an artist! When I was studying music therapy, in class one day we discussed various artists and music that was appealing and accurate, in terms of pitch, smooth airflow, bel canto, chiaroscuro, enunciation, and resonance. In essence, we were choosing artists who sang musically ideal, no gravelly voice or uneven pitch. It was a fascinating experience, as people voiced, one by one, their favorite musically accurate artist. Then I said Ben Harper, and the teacher looked at me for a moment before asking, why? The assignment, to me, meant who did I like the sound of. Ben Harper, a famous musician, actually has quite a gravelly voice, less than smooth pitch, and to everyone else in class, they couldn't understand why I would like that sound. It's similar to my question about why would anyone like the sound of Bob Dylan and his whine, no offense. With the technical measures of music and song, similar to all sentient beings, there can be a perfect pitch or harmony, and a less than perfect pitch. Of course, beauty is in the eyes or ears of the beholder, which is so awesome. Consider, there are three individuals who are meeting for the first time. Two individuals get along swimmingly with the third, but those same two individuals could, on the other hand, go without speaking to one another ever again. As in, they don't like one another, they don't resonate. Resonance. What and who resonates with you now in life is likely different than what and who resonated with you 10 years ago, due to your own internal changes. Like attracts like. Similar individuals come together, and you could say karmic experiences occur sometimes repeatedly with new individuals, say three times, until we recognize and realize the truth or lesson in the repeat experience. Once we are aware, we shift, choose differently, and likely no longer attract that same energy. Time for an upgrade!

So, I chose the artist I liked the sound of, at that time in my life. Nothing personal, but I no longer enjoy the sound of that artist, and haven't for several years. This is not just due to the sound of his voice, but the overall resonance of his music, that I no longer feel drawn to listen to. I correlate his music to a melancholic state, which I don't enjoy inducing anymore. You reading this book, perhaps, you already have an intuitive, natural sense about you, that you jive with certain things and not with others. You attract similar relationships over time, and you may even say, this or that resonates, and that doesn't resonate. What I mean when I make that statement is, I am in a similar vibrational frequency, resonance, or harmonic resonance with an individual, thing, place, or experience. While there are measurable tools to assess our various individual electromagnetic frequency, brain wave activity in hertz, etc., at any given moment, we can use something far more sophisticated to measure whether we jive with someone, something, or not. It's our own internal feelings, perhaps a feeling in our gut, our chest, our entire body, or noticing how our mood is affected by listening to a person, listening to a certain type of music, or hearing a song we would rather never hear again in our lives. We are sophisticated beings, subconsciously and consciously aware of what feels good, who we love being around, and what we like to listen to.

I love the topic of resonance because when individuals I work with begin to become free from disease, their own frequency changes, and when this occurs, things they used to be okay with—people, relationships, foods, locations, what have you, that they used to want to engage with—will often shift or change completely. The simplest way of stating this is, they no longer resonate with what they did when they were sick. It's not shocking, yet, it is profound. When you are your true, resonant, centered, authentic Self, soul Self, you cannot carry around a chronic disease, you aren't carrying around a false or old story, you are living in the Now and you are free to Be the true you. Freedom from disease is freedom from All that you are Not. When you are free from disease, you no longer resonate with that which is a lie, which creates dissonance within you. You choose out of pure recognition, root and soul vibration, to return to balance, return to harmony, to release yourself from what you recognize as lies, and from what holds you back from Truth and Freedom. Similarly said, once you know the truth, it cannot be unknown.

Music can move us to tears in a moment, recall a memory within a flash, and get us moving our body from stillness within a second. Music is either a good vibration or lesser. We create our own music, our own song, some say, by our life, and I believe we create many songs, different movements all together creating a symphony, similar to Indian ragas. There are typically four ragas in Hindu classical music, like chapters to our lives. Are you creating a harmonious symphony of body, mind, heart, and spirit? No judgment, no need for more judgment, shame, or blame if you don't like the song. If you enjoy the song, the harmony of your own tune, with joy, then please carry on making that music. Yet, if you feel your own orchestra is playing a mess of a song, chaotic, off-beat, out of tune, then, by all means, let that bad dream go. Start anew, this very moment, for the creation of a beautiful song. Internal harmony is possible. It is a choice, and just like a classic piano, we ask a professional tuner to come in and masterfully tune the pads and strings. This is perfectly fine, after all you are still the one creating the song, playing the notes and chords, healing your body, experiencing your experience, just not alone, never alone.

In the early 1980s, Fabien Maman, one of the leading experts on vibrational sound healing, studied the human cell at the University of Jussieu, Paris, France. He photographed cells as they were exposed to acoustic sounds, using a Kirlian camera, which captures the coronal discharges around an object. A coronal discharge is an electrical discharge caused by the ionization of gas or fluid surrounding an object. In this way, he visually demonstrated the positive effects of favorable frequencies on cells. He realized that each cell had vibrational affinity to certain notes, and when that note was played, the photographed image showed a beautiful mandala shape emanating pinks and blues. His studies demonstrated what we now know, that cells and therefore organs and glands, variable throughout the body, have preferable notes and harmonics which when they "hear" or vibrate to those frequencies, create harmony. Hence, using vibrational healing modalities, not only music, to tune and harmonize the body, begins at the cellular level, or arguably at the quantum level.

Think about how your body feels, how you feel when you hear a song, or music that is peaceful and calming to your nervous system? Now think about music, or sounds, like loud roaring vehicles continuously driving by, which cause you irritation or rub on your nerves. There is a reason that various music causes varied responses in each person, which I will explain further on. The basics are healing the cells, creating resonance in the body, harmony from the cells to the organs to the entire body, including the nervous system, begins and ends with frequency, vibration. Is it really as simple as listening to your favorite music though? Ultimately, his work and those that followed have shown us visually, like nature herself does, that when there are harmonious sounds, there are harmonious waves, frequencies, and healing naturally occurs.

In my work with individuals, the effects of vibration always come into conversation. I share the following. The body is like an orchestra, with the various organs, glands, and energy bodies being various instruments of the orchestra. When there is dis-ease in the body, then these various instruments are out of tune, playing the wrong note, or off tempo. So therefore, healing is the tuning and harmonizing of the individual instruments of the entire orchestra. One's entire being, made of the physical body, emotions, mental, spiritual, and vibrational being are capable of creating a most beautiful symphony when the instruments are in tune, in harmony. Closing your eyes, can you imagine your body as a glorious symphony; can you hear the harmony? When I close my eyes and take a few breaths, I hear a most unique song. Sometimes the song is like the wind, peaceful and calm. Other times there is a bounding bubbly jazz, bluegrass, reggae conglomeration playing in joyous harmony, of course. As we evolve on the journey to health, we can hear this internal song, because we are in tune, and it will be a unique expression for each of us, a song never played in quite this way before. It rises and flows like a living, loving river.

Another metaphor passed along from my mentor, Dr. Dickson Thom, DDS, ND, is the River of Health. Imagine when we are born we are born in the crystal clear blue waters of a mountain spring, atop a pristine mountain of beauty. Life occurs and through experiences such as trauma, illness, and suppression, the source spring becomes farther away, upstream as it were. This is because the being is making adaptations to survive, to do the best it can, given the circumstances it is presented with, and in the ways it is taught to respond. When individuals come to meet me, often in the midst of a chronic illness, they are in essence, in the murky downstream waters, where there isn't smooth or clear flowing waters anymore, and there is perhaps trash or dead aquatic life floating in the water. There is stagnation at best, and sometimes they are in swift rapids being carried downriver. So, our intention, with everyone, is to assist in restoring one's innate right to health and vitality, to return to the crystal clear blue waters of the mountain spring. It could be argued, quite honestly, that the clear, crystal, blue-green water is not where every individual begins their physical existence. Due to epigenetics, we know that what occurs in the life of your paternal and maternal lineage at least three generations ago, has the potential of affecting your health today. It is common to see the experiences of a grandparent affecting the experience of their grandchild in my practice. Whatever your mother's health was, mentally and emotionally throughout her pregnancy and delivery with you, affects the energetic and physical foundation of you as a baby. This factor often leaves mothers and also fathers, because although they do not carry the baby, their health has an effect also, feeling as though they have done something wrong, or wishing they knew then what they know now so they would have made different choices. What I say to them is, we are all always doing our best from what we know, and we choose differently when we know to do so. This life is a journey, and in my experience, healing one generation allows for generational healing, or what some refer to as ancestral healing. Due to the effects of epigenetics, harmful subconscious programming that gets passed down through generations, I am especially passionate about working with individuals prior to conceptions in order to optimize their health and harmonize their whole being prior to bringing new life in. Wherever an individual is at, whatever their age, there is always hope and potential to heal, and whenever that intention is set, it is perfect. Be Here Now.

While in college for music therapy, we brought our instruments and voices to various settings, including nursing homes, a juvenile detention center, and local hospital. We made rain sticks, sang songs, drummed drums, shared in memories and laughter, and brought vibrations of joy, healing, and peace to the humans who were "shut-in." Their eyes lit up, smiles grew, toes tapped, hands clapped, bodies swayed, and tears flowed. Music touches the soul. When patients work with me for the purpose of reversing disease, especially autoimmune diseases, completely, and we get to the phase of clearing the subconscious programming that causes the perpetuation of beliefs and therefore illness. During that phase especially, the various chords related to the associated chakras are utilized, as are color swatches, which can be placed or worn over the respective chakras or organs. Basic treatment guidelines include vibrational modalities, such as harmonics, flower essences, colors frequencies, clothing, foods, visualizations, homeopathics, organotherapies, oligotherapies, cell salts, expressions, etc, etc. In this way, when we work with the most subtle medicine, after the physical and emotional bodies have been supported to respond with vitality and trust, the subtle medicines are able to provide profound, profound healing, within an instant. This is where I see the living example that the physical is not the physical. This came from my own near death experience. While experiencing the symptoms of a full on heart attack, I did leave my body while experiencing excruciating pain throughout my body. I returned, having chosen Love, and within a moment, excruciating pain became blissful aliveness, like liquid light and love pulsing through my being. The physical is not the physical.

Everything is vibration. Everything is energy in a varied degree of motion. Whether it be trees silently drawing water up through their roots to their uppermost leaves, or your body's cells opening and closing to allow nutrients in and waste out. Nerve signals, one of the major ways of communication and function throughout the body, are controlled by the nervous system, a series of electrical, energetic signaling. There are glandular secretions occurring regularly, which are a cascade of responses to other glands, but also thoughts, smells, and intentions. For example, when you smell food, in a relaxed environment, you may realize that you are now hungry. Simply thinking about eating with the slightest sense of appetite, signals your salivary glands to begin secreting saliva. Saliva is the mixture of clear fluids from the parotid, sublingual, and submandibular salivary glands, which moistens the mouth and assists in the breakdown of food, starting in the mouth, with active enzymes, such as amylase. Remember this can happen simply from thinking about food, smelling food, or talking about food, before food is even tasted. Similarly, the effect of smiling, even when you don't feel like smiling naturally, your body responds to the smile by releasing "happy hormones," similarly to positive intention and thought.

There is an innate healing power within the body, and since my own youth I have understood that the healing power of nature was the most powerful in healing and balancing the body, mind, and spirit. There is no substitute for nature, naturally, this is not shocking.

I could write and speak about vibration, resonance, frequency, quantum reality, healing, music, truth, and Love forever. From my perspective, my love for vibration and resonance is, in essence, why I was called into *Sacred Connection*. Ann expressed her calling to create *Sacred Connection*, and I have enjoyed witnessing and communing with light-minded individuals, as we share our life experiences and passions with one another in alignment with truth, for the freedom of body, mind, and spirit. The *Sacred Connection* journey is one I am honored and have the pleasure of being witness and co-creatress to while co-hosting, writing, and weaving it through my own life. For where truth is the way, then light is the path. To all who have come before, and those who are yet to come, I offer the remembrance of these words. *Everything is music, the physical isn't the physical,* and when you are your true Self, your soul Self, you are free within body, mind, heart, and spirit.

If you would like to continue a conversation with me in any sense of the word, or you are considering healing support for yourself or someone you love, you can schedule a complimentary exploration call with me through my website at vitalityhealingnd.com or explore the various way to connect with me through my Linktree below, Blessed Be.

linktr.ee/drmarkham

Dr. Jennifer Markham, ND

Maurine Xavier

Maurine Xavier is a Breakthrough Mentor and Divine Guide who supports women to have more fun, freedom and flow. She is an expert in Transformational Leadership, spirituality, & channeling Divine Guidance. She also has three decades experience as a CPA, financial executive & wellness entrepreneur. Women partnering with her feel lighter, more confident and spontaneously manifest their ideal clients, co-creators and cash flow.

A STORY OF TURNING POINTS & TRANSFORMATION

by Maurine Xavier

Welcome to a story my soul wanted me to tell, my story of *Sacred Connection*. This story includes connection, disconnection and reconnection to the True and eternal me. My story is one of breaking down, breaking open, and breaking through.

I've had many pivotal moments in my life. The journey to tell this story is one of them. It was a journey of creation moving through me. In that space, I noticed I was disconnected from telling this story because I had fears of what could happen if I was truthful with myself and with you about my life. My ego and my history initially got in the way of me writing a heart inspired story. My soul held the space for me to discover and tell this story, a story of heartache, transformation, and truth.

My story of *Sacred Connection* invites you to connect and discover where you have disconnected from Truth. Your mind might want to get in the way of you doing that. It's okay. If your mind gets in the way, consider these tools to connect and reconnect to yourself and to what I am sharing.

If your mind wanders, notice it. Get curious about where it's wandering. Be open to being the space where it wanders and the space you reconnect.

If your mind shuts down, allow it to shut. If you start noticing resistance to what I am saying, have space for resistance. Be open to allowing all of your resistance and the story to be here too. Ask yourself questions like: Am I hiding from something I don't want to see? Is this resistance here to protect me? Is there something for me to know and take a deeper look at? Be willing and open to allowing it all to be here with you as you read. Take a deep breath. Take notes on what you discover. Be willing to allow your Self and all limited selves too. Take a break and come back when you are open.

My hope for you is that you find inspiration, connect with a possibility you haven't considered, and connect to a deeper level of you than ever before.

Are you willing to break apart the parts of you that want to break open?

Are you willing to break open to living a new possibility for your life?

Are you willing to live love now?

If you are, say aloud...

I am willing to break apart what doesn't work and open to what does.

I am willing to break open and live the Truth I Am.

I am willing to Be I Am.

LITTLE MAURINE

While growing up, I ran. I ran for love. I ran for straight As. I ran for cheerleader. I ran to keep up. Although I didn't know it, most of my running was to be who I was and who I wasn't.

Most of the time, I was anxious. I sucked my thumb. I wet my pants. I was outspoken. I had a hard time reading, and I was brilliant in math.

My parents drank, yelled, and cursed. I got scared when they drank, and they often drank too much. They fought. I fought. We fought about everything, just about. I was uncomfortable. Sometimes I watched people being hit, and sometimes I imagined myself being hit for things I didn't understand. I learned to compensate for what was going on around me by thinking and feeling very deeply.

I felt what people were thinking. I felt the room around me. I was hyperaware of what was going on around me, always on the lookout for something to fix. It felt good to fix.

One day when I was three years old, I heard a lot of hitting in the other room. It scared me. In the moment, hearing what was going on, I wanted to die. I wanted to leave the planet. I wanted to be taken home to a place where I was safe. I completely left my body. The words I heard and the intensity of emotion I felt from my parents felt scary. I was afraid for myself, and I was afraid for them. I was afraid they were going to die. THAT was really scary. How would I live if I didn't have a mom? I didn't know how to handle that thought and the feelings it provoked. I didn't even know I was thinking them. I simply was the thoughts and feelings I was having. In that moment, I left my body and never saw myself or my life in the same way.

Since I didn't leave the planet, I learned a new way to live. I developed a new sense of safety, one that was manufactured in my head. I call that sense of safety my "ego."

In general, egos are a support system for children. Egos are a normal and natural part of being human. Egos are thought forms. Egos are sub-selves created in the mind. Egos are built to create a parallel reality. They build shelter. They build support. They build something to rely on. Egos serve a purpose, especially when you have trauma like me.

Egos have a specific objective in mind. My ego was built to protect me. My ego was formed to create space for me to survive, when I believed like truth I wasn't safe, and when I believed, I wasn't safe having the feelings I had about my parents' fight. My ego helped me continue to live through that moment when I wanted to die. In that moment, my "ego" became a self who took over my reality and my life. I disconnected from the True Self, even more than I already had. I became attached to this ego to be safe, to survive, and to be alive.

I didn't know I built an ego. It just happened. That's what egos do, especially in situations like these. They are automatic survival mechanisms that create safety around something that doesn't appear safe. I became my ego, and I believed unconsciously it was me.

Having intense feelings, specifically feelings of fear, were not new for me. I had already survived fear, many times before. I had come back to the Earth for this incarnation to be love and to survive fear in a new way, a way that didn't require ego to keep me safe. Prior lives, and my relationship with fear, impacted the way I survived this childhood experience.

Even though I didn't know it until I was fifty, I had already chosen to live where there was violence. I had lessons to learn, and I came to learn them with these people and with fear. To the infinite me who has made decisions about many things, safety involved violence. Safety involved being a victim. Safety involved being humiliated. Safety involved playing the savior.

This time, and in that moment, I decided to "be" the one who would keep everyone safe. I decided to play a role I already knew. I returned to "being the savior".

Life as a savior takes on many different roles and responsibilities. Life for me, as the savior, looked like this:

- Sacrificing myself for others
- Looking to and for people to save
- Expecting myself to be a savior
- Taking responsibility for other people's lives
- Neglecting my needs
- Putting my needs last

I did a bang-up job being the savior.

I started feeling and processing energy in the space, as a way to feel comfortable. I made my mom the one I needed to save. I also made her the one I needed to keep safe. I put my needs last, without even knowing it. I honestly didn't even know myself well enough to know who I was or what I was feeling. I assumed everything I felt was me, which made for a very muddy life and made it impossible to know what energy or need was mine and what wasn't. Some of what I experienced could be called codependency or being an empath. I say it's WAY deeper than that. I call it Little Maurine being totally and completely lost in a coping mechanism and having absolutely no idea I was lost.

I became an overachiever. I also became someone who stuffed my feelings. I "was" someone who looked to other people before being me.

I drank my first drink at eight when I spiked my orange juice with vodka. I was bulimic at eleven. I would binge eat to soothe my pain and throw up to release what didn't feel good. I started binge drinking at fourteen when everything became too stressful and hard. I was a workaholic starting in my late teens. I was obsessed with having enough money to survive and saw earning money as my ticket to freedom. I used work to avoid my feelings and the fact that I thought (no I "was") being the hero, the helper and the savior was normal.

I was also funny, kind and cute. I loved to bake. I was a cheerleader, a prom queen candidate, and a great friend. I loved to dance and wanted to be a Solid Gold dancer.

I had a remarkably successful career in public accounting and as a financial executive. I attracted my husband, who I sensed would be my husband two days after we met. He could handle my sarcasm, my strong tongue, and he was a Catholic. Who could ask for more?! Everything looked great on the outside. On the inside, I was addicted, disconnected to my ground of well-being, and totally lost in not knowing who I am.

TURNING POINTS

I had my first turning point in 1996. I was thirty-three and ten months into being a stay-at-home mom. I had retired myself from a high profile, exciting and well-paying job as Division Controller and Director of Wholesale Operations for Esprit de Corp, (the Taylor Swift of junior clothing in the 1980s). I left my career because I had an intuition that I was going to get fired if I didn't leave. I was burnt out from burning the candle at both ends, and I was lucky enough to become a stay-at-home mom when my son was twenty months old.

My son was just short of three-years-old, and my daughter was five months old. My daughter would not wean to a bottle, and she was waking up every two hours throughout the night. I was obsessively on the go, entertaining my children. I was exhausted. I can remember lying in my bed at nine o'clock one evening. The house was quiet and still. Both of my kids were asleep. I couldn't deal with the fact that I had no control over when I would need to get up to breast feed her. I was beside myself that I couldn't predict when she would wake up or how long we would be awake. The thought of doing this all over again tomorrow was more than I could bear.

I was filled with dread and an impending sense of doom. My mind was racing. I felt anxiety in every cell of my being. I felt like the world was closing in on me. Eventually, the feelings dissipated, and I went to sleep.

Feeling like this was a turning point for me. During the day when I was busy, I felt less anxious, and I still had no idea how to deal with my underlying fear, anxiety and exhaustion. I had been avoiding seeing a therapist for years and, within a week, I knew it was time to take the plunge and ask for help.

That decision led to me starting individual and group therapy. Within three months, I started taking antidepressants, which helped me with my obsessive tendencies, chronic depression, and anxiety disorder. The combination of therapy and biochemical support was hugely helpful. I started to connect to "the real world". I also started connecting the dots to what was real and what was made up.

I continued therapy for fifteen years, including bouts of couples counseling too. Antidepressants were a lifeline to feeling better. I became acquainted with a sense of self that I was disconnected from and did not know in my body. Even though my husband gave me a hard time for being in so much therapy and disagreed with my taking antidepressants, I knew DEEP DOWN I was on the right track. I knew I deserved to be happy, and I wasn't going to stop until I found what I was looking for.

Between 1996 and 2011, I experienced many major breakthroughs. Being a parent helped me connect to my inner child. Being a wife and a mother allowed me to find strength, courage, and innate knowing. Leaping into network marketing, with the desire to help people become physically, financially, and emotionally free, showed me what it was like to follow my heart in business. My father's passing away gave me space to see, be and feel repressed emotions, that I had been hiding from. I was ready for more. I was ready to take the next steps into a more fulfilling life. Although I didn't know how, I had faith, the steps would be presented to me.

In October 2010, I met Dr. David Kamnitzer at a network marketing event. Dr. David was one of the presenters, a Wholistic Chiropractor and a natural healing expert. He had some handouts, and I answered questions about what I wanted in life. I thought nothing of it and went about my business. He called me a couple times telling me he could help me have what I wanted, which was peace of mind and more freedom. I said no to his invitations because I was done investing in teachers and programs. It was time to stand on my own two feet and do what I already knew.

In February 2011, Dr. David called me a third time. I hesitated to answer the phone because I thought it was another sales call. I answered anyway. I will never forget. It was two o'clock. I was sitting at a white corner desk in my home office. I was facing the wall, and the light was muted. I picked up the phone and said, "Hello." He said, "Hello." We had some small talk. Then he said, "Spirit asked me to reach out to you again."

I had planned to say no to whatever he was offering. When he said that, I was stopped in my tracks. I took a deep breath. Part of me was with him, and part of me had left the building. I can still feel it in my body. I was flushed, almost embarrassed. I felt like he knew more than me. I was ready to say no… again. Then it hit me. I have been praying for peace of mind, for a really long time. I had been in Adult Children of Alcoholics, a 12 Step Program, for six months. I was committedly doing the steps. Step 2 is, "Came to believe that a power greater than ourselves could restore us to sanity." Step 3 is, "Made a decision to turn our will and our lives over to the care of God as we understand God." My head dropped back. I looked towards heaven. I had this flush of energy run through my body. I said to myself, "This is what you have been praying for. God sent him." I said yes to meeting with him.

Two weeks later and a week after my mother passed away, we had our first session. I already knew I was here for a bigger plan. When I sat down in front of him, I felt what I imagined "real love" feels like. I felt safe. I felt calm. I felt there was space for me to be me. I didn't know what the journey was, and I knew it was something new.

Three weeks into working together, he asked me to commit at a deeper level, to living transformation. He told me he was taking me on a one-way journey, a journey from which I would never recover. While I didn't "get" living transformation, I had already experienced shifts in my ground of being. I liked what I was experiencing and wanted more.

According to Dr. David, "Transformation is a body of distinctions, a set of practices, and method for reliably gaining access to what you don't know you don't know, the knowing of which could make a big difference both in the quality of your life and in your effectiveness in life."

Did I just blow your mind? Yep, I get it. Hang in here with me.

According to Merriam Webster Dictionary:

- **Transformation** means to change completely in composition, structure, or character, and to change in outward appearance.
- **Distinction** means the act of perceiving someone or something as being not the same and often treating as separate or different, something that distinguishes, and the quality or state of being excellent or superior.

To me, transformation is a possibility you live, that provides space for you to be, unfold, accept and allow all that is here now, all that has been, and all that will be. Transformation is "shifting your relationship with" what is, including you, your thoughts, feelings, experiences, memories, and ways of being. Transformation supports you to reconnect to the True You, your infinite being, authentic expression, and I Am presence.

With this story, I intend to build a bridge from Dr. David's definition of transformation to what I experienced as his student. When I met Dr. David, I was running around in a maze of thoughts, feelings, and experiences. I was trying to predict, control, and manage my life and others lives too. I was overwhelmed a lot. I was overcommitted and obsessed by doing. I was usually late and beat myself up about it. While I knew my life would be easier if I did less and listened to my intuition more, I rarely did. It was somehow more satisfying to keep doing and be late. My body felt stiff as a board. My nerves were on edge. I would have a massage, relax, and return to feeling like a stress ball quickly after I left the treatment room.

TRANSFORMATION IS A BODY OF DISTINCTIONS

One of the distinctions Dr. David taught me is, "I Am prior to and senior to my thoughts. I Am prior to and senior to my feelings. I Am prior to and senior to my experiences."

Be with these sentences now. "I Am prior to and senior to my thoughts. I Am prior and senior to my feelings. I Am prior to and senior to my experiences."

Being with these ideas supported me to imagine that thoughts, feelings, experiences and me are unique spaces. I could imagine space for me, space for what I think, space for what I feel, and space for what I experience. I could also imagine there being space for all these to simultaneously coexist. I could imagine there was "space for me to be." I could conceive space to "have" thoughts, feelings, and experiences. It opened space for me to "have" awareness of thoughts, feelings and experiences as well. Having awareness gave me a whole new outlook on life. There was space to be and space to do. There was space for me to be before I had to do. I became aware of my being. There was space for me to choose before acting. There was space for me to consider doing and why I was doing what I was doing. There was space for me to stop "doing" as a way of feeling better.

This distinction introduced me to infinite spaciousness. Halleluia! I didn't have any idea space existed beyond what I felt. I no longer needed to race around avoiding my feelings or my thoughts. I had space for Little Maurine's repressed feelings and thoughts. She could now imagine it was possible to feel her anger and her pain without exploding. I had space to reconnect to Little Maurine. She started trusting me with her thoughts and feelings. Little Maurine's feelings started coming to the surface. The Universe brought me waves of energy I could handle. The True Little Maurine started to emerge from "ego".

My body started feeling better. I was allowing more and resisting less. My mind didn't have to be in control. My feelings were no longer responsible for me or my actions. I was. My body didn't have to let me know, as much as it did before, that I was trying to shove me into something I thought. My body had more space to flow with what's here.

TRANSFORMATION IS A SET OF PRACTICES

When you learn to play basketball, you are introduced to basketball and the fundamentals of playing basketball. You are introduced to concepts about basketball, and you play the game of basketball. Transformation works the same way.

Transformation is a set of distinctions that open you up to new ways of being and give you new frameworks for living. It's also a method of practices that support you to live outside the box. Transformation introduces you to being an infinite Being. Since being is in the domain of truth. You need to discover what truth is. There are a whole set of practices for that. The process of discovery involves learning "what you don't know you don't know."

Transformation includes, "the practice of creating more space for you to be."

Imagine what it feels like to be six feet four inches tall, weighing three hundred pounds, and be sitting in a middle seat in coach class for a six-hour flight. When I imagine that, I feel cramped. I feel like holding my breath. My shoulders slump. My knees start to cramp. I don't have space to move my legs. My head is pulsating. I think, "F*&ck this sh*t. How long do I have to sit this way?"

This is a thought experiment to introduce you to ideas about what transformation can do for you. The thought of being six feet four inches tall and shoving myself into a middle seat for six hours is what we do to ourselves when we decide to be ego and the space ego is. Ego "is" a thought experiment we got lost in.

"Creating more space to be" involved activities and experiments where Dr. David introduced me to ways of being where I could imagine myself to "be" beyond thoughts and feelings that held me back and simply weren't true. There is a set of practices Dr. David used to support me to transform out of being thoughts, feelings, and experiences and into being an infinite Being having a human experience.

My favorite tool for creating more space is "what if questions." What if questions invited me to step into an idea, like a possibility, to see what I saw, to feel what I felt, to notice what I noticed, and to simply be without having to find an answer. It's a curiosity and a consideration. Stepping into what if questions gave my mind a space to imagine. What if questions gave my body space beyond the thought of the body, which naturally created space for me to breathe more deeply and relax.

Creating space for me to make decisions was crucial. I didn't know there was space to decide. I just did. Creating space for me to "be" was necessary for me to have peace of mind. The practice included what if questions.

One of the questions I would invite my "doer" into is, "*What if you gave yourself permission to do less? Is that possible for you?*" I would ask her to pay attention to what happens in her body. If she relaxed, I would ask her if she would like to relax more. If the idea of relaxing was challenging, I would ask her to consider what relaxing means to her. We would continue on this path until she had a breakthrough, or we would stop when she was ready.

The intention of what if questions is to open the mind to considering new options, and, in the space of new options, there is more freedom. Creating more space to be opened me to having more freedom, and that felt really good!

TRANSFORMATION IS A METHOD

According to Dr. David Kamnitzer, "Transformation is a method for reliably gaining access to what you don't know you don't know, the knowing of which could make a big difference both in the quality of your life and in your effectiveness in life." In my opinion, Transformation itself is an intuitive process. It's a connection to grace. It's a space to be and a space to open up to more of what is. The method Dr. David used was fueled by his intuition, his mastery, his desire to serve, and by what I was desiring. He used all these to create methods and practices that suited a higher purpose.

The method of Transformation is allowing what wants to happen to unfold in time and space and being the conduit for the Universe to connect me to the path of Truth. The intent and overall desires I had were to feel better, to be happy, and to have more freedom. That was the context for our work together, and it worked!

Within three months of being his client and student, I knew I was ready to complete therapy. Psychology broke open that I had a dysfunctional childhood. Therapy helped me see how unreasonable I was being with myself. Therapy helped me build a new relationship with myself. Psychology was an entry point for me to discover my True self as well as the one I had left behind.

Transformation was the next step to me discovering who I Truly Am. Transformation and working with Dr. David as my spiritual teacher, ontological coach, and modern-day mystic supported me to move beyond "being" the savior in my family and being "the savior" period.

The path of transformation is eternal. It's one that never completes. It's one I am still living. I got to the point where I knew too much about who I am, to ever return to not knowing. Yet I wasn't ready to take the next leap of faith to "be" love, having a human experience.

BREAKING POINT

It was 2015. Four years into being Dr. David's student, I had one foot on the dock, holding on tight to the control I found in story, and holding on tight to ego as me. I had the other foot on the boat, representing faith in the eternal now, faith in me as love, and faith in Creator as my source. I lived with one foot on the dock and one foot on the boat for nineteen months.

I had already gone back to work in accounting. I was living a life fueled by fear and by the angst, "I'm not doing enough." I had fear of money steeped in my body and in my history. I "was" not enough money to survive, which was my mother's energy from the womb. I felt guilty and ashamed. I was trying to save face. I was also lost in belief systems of my ancestors, 3rd Dimension programming, and patterns of being a woman.

I was disconnected from Source. I was hopeless. I became suicidal. Even though I still met with Dr. David weekly, I had disconnected from the teachings. I was choosing "my path." I was neglecting my soul's path. While it wasn't visible to me, I was denying my Creator. I "was" denying myself. I "was" I wasn't worthy. I "was" I had denied love. I was also blind to all of that. It was a part of what I didn't know I didn't know. At the time, it was too scary to see and too scary to reconcile with. I wasn't yet willing to fully connect to love as my path. It took a deeper level of commitment than I was ready to make at the time.

My soul was calling me forward, and my ego was calling me back. I felt stretched and pulled apart, figuratively and literally. My soul had a message and a vision for me, and I wasn't ready to hear it. The message was, "Be a Transformational Leader. Allow yourself to know the truth of God and share it throughout the world." Although I had no idea this was happening, I was afraid of what that meant. I was afraid I would relive the past. I was afraid I would "be" that person I was meant to be, and it would disrupt the family organization I came from. I hadn't yet moved on beyond Little Maurine's pictures of life, her fears, her memories, her desperation, and her covenant with Creator. Little Maurine was entangled in prior life decisions, "I won't be THAT woman. I won't be the Spirit moving through me. I won't go from town to town sharing the message of Your will. I won't die on the cross like Jesus did. I saw how much it hurt his family, and I am afraid that will happen to me, right here and right now."

This was the invisible knowledge I was telling myself. I had made a covenant with God to never come back and do His work, and I was living out that covenant in the background of my life. I "was" that covenant. This covenant and belief systems in general were the dock I was holding on to. I would never let myself suffer again for His will. I chose that. That choice held me back. That choice was my life. I was creating suffering now because of a covenant I had previously made that I didn't know I had made. The energy, my soul's path, the energy and momentum Dr. David created with me, the things I had learned about me and life, the opportunities grace had for me, and life itself, combined with the covenants I had created for myself were a no-win situation. It was impossible to serve those covenants and my Creator at the same time.

I grew weary. I grew desperate. I grew afraid. I had withdrawn from my social circle. I had become a horrible partner to my husband. I was working, and that was it. What was I working for, a short-term solution to my problems, the fear I had about money, and the faith I had in money being my savior? I was ashamed of myself. I was living the life of Christ in my head over and over and over again in another dimension of consciousness. That's why I was holding myself back. I saw Him die on the cross, and I thought that was going to be me if I stepped forward. NONE of this was conscious at the time. It was in the realm of what I didn't know I didn't know, and I was NOT willing to discover more about Truth then.

BREAKING THROUGH

I was in my car on the way to work. I wanted to die, as I had for months. I was more committed to death and dying than I was to moving forward. Death to me was life. Death to me was freeing myself from the body I thought was the cause of my problems. That was until I decided that I wanted something else. This day in April 2016, I finally was willing to have more. I reconnected to why I had started working with Dr. David in the first place.

Sincerely and humbly, I called Dr. David and told him how desperate I was. I told him how deeply I was considering suicide and how I wanted a new solution. He asked me, "Do you really want to commit suicide?" I said, "Of course not." I didn't WANT to commit suicide. It was the only option I had for getting out of pain. He told me, "Just because you leave your body doesn't mean you're going to be out of pain."

What I really wanted was to get out of pain, and leaving my body was the only way I knew how to do that at the time. At that moment, I discovered something I didn't know I didn't know. I didn't realize that I had been being, "Bodies are me, and I am my pain." I had been in pain my whole life, one way or the other. That was the sub context for my life, and it had come to the surface through this experience and this awareness. I had been living a fantasy about the body and a fantasy about me as pain. These were connected. Dr. David helped me break them apart and connect to what's true. Bodies are not pain, so leaving a body doesn't solve the problem, I am in pain. I immediately and permanently broke open. I never again considered suicide as a pathway to feel good. It was no longer even on the map.

That day, I broke open to a sea of endless possibilities, and I have been living as the sea of endless possibilities ever since. I was introduced to new teachers and teachings that are a part of my soul's greater and plan. I was called to learn how to channel Divine Guidance. I went through a radical spiritual awakening that left me being a Divine Guide. I evolved and I was ready to be of service in a Divinely Guided way. I trusted myself enough to quit my accounting job and allow myself to be abundant with and without an income. In March 2017, I started my own business as a Breakthrough Mentor, Transformational Leader and Divine Guide.

My soul asked me to write this story so that I may know myself beyond story. It was a journey of awakening and VERY DEEP transformation. The difference between "me" now, the me who is writing the story, and "the savior me", the "doer me", and the "suicidal me" is: I Am (period). I have unshakeable faith in me, *I Am*. I Am inseparable from God. I Am God itself, an aspect of God that is also God.

I still get lost in my thoughts. I still "am" my stories, sometimes. I laugh at myself when I find myself lost in ego. I continue to be shocked by Truth. I am grounded enough in Truth to discover when I am off base and to discover the truth of it at the same time. I am still living the same life I was always living. My relationship with my thinking mind has changed. That's it.

I am walking the path of love and light.

I have manifested my dream life, my dream home, and the husband I always wanted. My husband is the same man I married in 1988. As I have become the love of my life, I could be with him in a way that invites him to love me back. It wasn't easy and it wasn't fast. I had burned a lot of bridges with him over the years. He had a lot of scars about me, and he didn't trust me. I also didn't trust myself, and it was coming through in him. In November 2019, he took me up on the invitation to love me and trust me now. This experience was a real test for how committed I was to love, win-win realities, and living transformation at the level of relationship.

As of November 2023, I live in the Central Coast of California, fifteen minutes from the Pacific Ocean. I go on adventures in the trees and near the ocean as often as I choose. I completely trust I deserve this comfort and will always have access to a comfortable life. I have a transformed relationship with my body. My eating addiction and my hatred of my body have disappeared. While I still have eating issues, I have a healthy relationship with food and drink. I love myself and my body. I have been off antidepressant medications since December 2017. I have the ability to handle intense emotions. The energy enters my space. I allow myself to be present with what's present. I breathe deeply. I "be with" what's here. I keep breathing. I relax. I pay attention to what I am thinking. I open my heart. I allow it to support me. I release what's present, and the energy passes.

I am a lightning rod for miracles. Since 2017, I have helped hundreds of women personally and through my business, Beacon of Light with Maurine Xavier. I am paying forward what I learned from Dr. David Kamnitzer, utilizing a combination of my unique gifts and talents and Transformation. I channel guidance from an ever-expanding team of Divine Guides. I have embraced myself as a wise woman with divine intelligence equal to the Divine Guides I channel. I use a co-creative technology, The Diamond Co-Creative System®, to bridge science to spirituality. Using The System, I support myself and my clients to accelerate personal awareness, transformation and evolution, to open and expand awareness, intuition, and gifts, and to heal, realign, and update our frequency and DNA patterns into 5th Dimension and higher.

I am a master at breaking apart my own sh*$t and am deeply committed to serving others who desire to be and do the same!

Living transformation isn't only for me. It's for anyone who chooses to live it!

Transformation is a pathway for me and those I serve. The women I support, have a new level of mastery in their lives. They trust themselves more. They have more freedom and fun. They have released co-dependencies with family members. They have courage to say yes to their hearts and to say no to doing what other people think they should do. They have empowered relationships with themselves and with men too. They have access to more money and trust money is always there. They are living their purpose and their passions. They really enjoy their lives too. They are living the lives they Truly Desire!

What they desire serves as the catalyst for the work and play we do together. I act as a conduit for them to connect to their hearts, their wisdom, their innate gifts, their True Selves, and the reason they came to the planet. To the extent they are willing, we co-create miracles together.

What happened for me can happen for anyone!

Would you like to breakthrough?

Are you willing to break open?

Let's Connect! https://bit.ly/MaurineXavierConnect

Please use this link to set up a 30-minute complimentary zoom with me.

I would be blessed and honored to have the opportunity to connect with and serve you.

SECRETS TO SACRED CONNECTION

These are my secrets for connecting and reconnecting to the True Me.

- Keep being willing to expand myself

- Connect to and follow my heart
- Have faith in the unknown
- Trust my connection to God
- Access my intuition and follow it
- Always have a partner I can rely on, even if that partner is me
- Ask for help when I need it
- Allow myself to receive more than ever before
- Breathe deeply and often
- Be in nature often and connect for guidance
- Put my bare feet upon the Earth and feel the love and presence of Mother Gaia supporting me
- Be willing to invest money in my awakening
- Be willing to invest in myself
- Trust the money will come
- Tune into God
- Turn it over to God regularly
- Say yes to unconditionally loving me and other people
- Love, love, love and love some more

I love you.

Please reach out if you are moved and want to connect!

https://bit.ly/MaurineXavierConnect

Brenda L Balding RN, MA

Brenda L Balding RN, MA. Is a Spiritual Guide for Women Who Struggle With Food or Body Image, author, and energy healer.

Brenda devotes time every day to support and expand her own spiritual journey of discovery for health and healing. She aids others in their self-exploration by sharing her own experience related to food, food behaviors, body image, and spiritual connection.

6) THIRD EYE — INTUITION

SACRED DISCOVERY

Discovering Brenda: an ongoing road of sacred discovery and new shores

by Brenda L Balding RN, MA

"One doesn't discover new lands without consenting to lose site of the shore for a very long time."
—ANDRE GIDE

Curiosity, notice, willingness, wonder, honesty are all words that I believe and incorporate into each day to the best of my ability. It's about the ongoing discovery of Brenda, who I am, how I respond in given situations, whether or not I want to respond in that way, all in support of how I want to show up in the world—from an authentic heart of love. The more I am willing to let go of what I think I know, the more "new shores" in me and others I experience. The only way, for me, is to walk in an attitude of honest discovery and to be of service for my good, our good, and the highest good of all.

Who is Brenda and, from where does she come? I was blessed to be raised in the Pacific Northwest, eldest of seven, in a good Catholic home until I finished college at a Catholic university where I studied nursing. I had a deep feeling that something was missing in my life and did not know what it was.

Growing up as a kinesthetic in a family where hugs or physical caresses of affection were not given, led to different forms of soothing for me. My parents did not know how to show affection in a physical way. They showed their love for us by making sure we were safe, had enough to eat, got a good education, and enjoyed family interactions with cousins, grandparents, and music. Food and isolating myself with fantasy books became my source of soothing. It didn't help that sweets were given when we got hurt and when I was in the hospital for various surgeries during my childhood.

The discovery of a Divine, loving, energy that could soothe me more deeply than food was mind-blowing. It came into my consciousness when I was introduced to and worked a 12-step program related to food. The 12-step spiritual principles are how I live my life each day to the best of my ability. More on that later.

Lack of self-worth, fear, and unacknowledged core beliefs all play a part in my sacred discovery journey.

I went searching for what was missing—food, self-worth, and core beliefs got in the way.

STOP 1 – Completion of a Bachelor of Science in Nursing, first RN job in New York, Brooklyn VA hospital for one year, and a boy's camp in the Adirondacks for a summer as a camp nurse.

During my senior year of college, not being good enough showed up in my consciousness after my first sexual interaction with someone I believed cared about me for the long-term. I felt good and warm inside as I stood looking out of the window while he dressed. Then I heard, "you could stand to lose some weight." I shriveled up inside and just stood there believing I was not good enough as I was. My self-image was in pieces. I know now that what he said was more about him than me. I was 5'4" and about 130 pounds. I felt good in my body for the most part before this.

I chose New York instead of staying in San Francisco—where my family moved when I was a junior in college—because I knew that if I stayed home, I would never travel. I was a homebody and a caregiver, watching out for the "little ones" as my mom requested from the time I was 8. Making sure that everyone was OK. I knew the answer was not there.

At the VA, I worked the PM shift, gave backrubs, and realized that my hands would get very warm, and I was helping the patients in a way I did not understand—what was called "healing hands" in the 1970's. I would also sing or hum, which the patients found healing as well. The patients called me "the singing nurse." Music and singing have been a part of my life for as long as I can remember. There is a picture of me sitting at a piano with my hands on the keys when I was about one. I sang in many choirs and played cello in a youth symphony orchestra. Guitar was my friend when singing in folk masses at church. I knew that peace and relaxation came for me and others with music and song.

I did not consciously know what I was doing. It just felt right. I am now a level two Reiki Healer—it feels very familiar—using my "healing hands".

Stop 1 discovery reflection – I love learning from my past. What I realize is that some feelings I want to hang on to may not be in my best interest. Having that realization assists me to be present when I notice others are wanting to live in the past. I can then share how it helps me to bring what I learned into NOW. Slowly learning to let go.

STOP 2 – Six-week Europe tour with a friend. Then I lived in Florence, Italy for 8 months, taking art history classes and 'living'; touring, falling in love, making tough decisions that challenged my beliefs, and continued to search.

Music came with me via my guitar, which I still have. I discovered more about me and how I wanted to show up for me and others, but still not totally aware. I did identify an increase in knowingness along with an awareness of how much I like food, especially bread and sweet pastries, and how they soothe me when I am in emotional turmoil, or at least I believed that.

One of the things I discovered while traveling around Europe is that I loved taking photographs, especially of the nature I was experiencing. I found, and still experience today, that the wonder of nature's life cycle is very spiritual. What I noticed is that when I looked deeply at a picture that moved me, I sat with what I was feeling, which was new for me. What was it telling me? What about specific photographs moved me? I took more photos and continued to search, ask, and notice.

Stop 2 discovery reflection – I begin to ask myself questions about what moves me, what challenges me, what do I want to learn? I also began to be conscious of what I was learning. I have continued to ask myself tough questions and to ask them of others as well. They deepen my self-awareness.

STOP 3 – San Francisco VA hospital respiratory intensive care unit for three years on night shift.

My healing hands were in deep demand for patients and staff, especially the physician residents. I learned much about me and how I respond to emergent situations. Food became less important as my self-worth expanded.

During my down time, I loved to go to piano bars and sing. I would always end up with a line of drinks in front of me; the first real, the rest virgin. It was so fun and relaxing. I was not going to any church during this time. I was exploring things like EST, chakra healing, energy work, and other spiritual modalities, as I continued my sacred discovery journey. I continue to walk in nature with my camera.On one of my walks, I experienced the aurora borealis in Alaska. A grade school friend of mine and I took a ferry boat out of Seattle, visited some of the cities, and experienced the first aurora borealis of the year according to the locals. It was a spiritual experience for me, and I still feel it in my heart today.

I noticed I began to eat when I was lonely, stressed, or when tough emotions showed up. This got in the way of divine sacred connection I learned later. A core belief that the best way to handle tough emotions is to eat shows up as I'm not good enough to do any better. The not good enough core belief.

Stop 3 discovery reflection – My discovery over time is that food, especially carbs, puts me to sleep so I don't have to feel. Talk about going unconscious. Making good choices from this place is iffy at best. When I share this experience with others who are dealing with food issues, they are surprised that they are not alone. I also discovered that an experience that touches my heart and stays with me for life, like the aurora borealis, can be tapped into to connect with the divine any time.

STOP 4 – Marriage, birth, miscarriages, and divorce in Sonoma.

I met my husband at my favorite piano bar. He was whistling in tune to the music. I was more aware of my inner "knowing" by this time. I knew as I walked down the church aisle that the marriage would not last. It was not in me yet to say no at that time in my life. Another realization—I was getting married because a younger sister was already married and my husband needed my help, I thought, as a Vietnam veteran in pain. The caregiver, "have to make it better," part of me showed up in force.

During this time of growth, stress, and learning more about Brenda, I started turning to food even more for solace. This was not a clear "knowing" yet. Looking back, I had used food to soothe me for years. It did not start showing on my body until my pregnancy. My daughter arrived the day after my 27th birthday, a year and a half after my marriage. A miracle to me. I continued to attempt to heal my husband, encouraging him to get help for what we now know as PTSD. His anger was palpable and action-oriented (holes in doors and walls), though he never touched us in anger. Still, this led to some PTSD in me as I found out later.

As I continued my sacred discovery journey, I joined a group with an energy meditation teacher. Learning how to read energy in others was helpful to me as it helped me understand what I was experiencing when I used my hands and "sight" or "knowingness" to read and heal others. I felt more connected to Brenda and yet separate, not good enough or questioning if I was "doing it right." I also participated in a hospital based liquid weight loss program and got down to 125 pounds in an attempt to keep my husband. It didn't work. I still had food issues and emotional struggles not helped by the psychological meetings in the program. I had a good body image, yet I still craved carbs and used them to stuff down my feelings.

Two miscarriages in addition to my husband's ongoing anger and pain related to his experiences in Vietnam led to deeper fear for our safety. Alcohol and marijuana didn't help him as he hoped, just as food did not help me. I was calm on the outside and devastated on the inside, stuffing down my feelings of unworthiness with food to hide my feelings. I started having nightmares about what I would do *when* he left, not *if* he left. I knew in my head that my daughter and I would be fine. I had a good career to fall back on and was still working part-time, thus was known in the healthcare community.

It turned out that my husband was having an affair with my best friend and decided to divorce me after seven years and marry her. This was both hard and a gift as he took his anger and pain with him. He insisted that we sell the house, so that he could get a little bit of money from it. We had taken out loans against the house because of his excess spending. He chose not to have any custody of our daughter, so there were no fights over visitation. I allowed open visitation, which he did not take advantage of. Visitation with his daughter was arranged by both of her stepmoms. More heartache for me and more "stuffing" and feelings of not being good enough. How could I let that core belief continue to run me? Because I hadn't really identified it or dealt with it in a conscious healing way, I realize now.

My daughter and I moved into an apartment for the interim until I felt emotionally stable enough to decide what to do next. I was working two swing shifts and two graveyard shifts a week at the local hospital. Thank goodness for wonderful childcare. My daughter never knew if I would pick her up in the morning or at midnight. A change had to come when she went into grade school. I started looking for daytime jobs.

Stop 4 discovery reflection – In retrospect, my husband leaving was a gift. His choice hurt, but at the same time, gave me freedom from psychological and emotional abuse. Weight loss programs don't work for me unless I address the emotional and the spiritual components. Though still in discovery mode about food and core beliefs, I did start to live in gratitude.

STOP 5 – Back to San Francisco, which was the only place I could find a daytime job as my daughter was going into 1st grade. The job was at *Chinese Hospital* in ChinaTown as a head nurse and quality evaluation that led to many discoveries.

We lived with my parents for eighteen months and then I bought a condo in the same neighborhood. During all that time, I went to church with my parents and put my daughter into the Catholic school. I also did personal counseling for a time. My eating was less potent, although I continued to feel a hole in my connection with the Divine, my emotions, and my body.

Four years of working at *Chinese Hospital* led to another discovery and a small slice out of my self-worth. I was asked to resign or be fired. The staff had apparently complained that I was not helping them enough by 'doing my part'. This was news to me. I chose to resign at that time. The staff surprised me with a 24c gold bracelet at my last day party. I felt even more lost. What now?

Stop 5 discovery reflection – Good can come out of adversity. I learned that my attitude makes a difference in my energy and in life.

STOP 6 – Three months without a job, spending my savings, food stamps, mild depression, and daily job hunting occupied me. Hiding all my feelings from my daughter the best that I could was the second focus. Food continued to soothe me, I thought. The job that found me was at a nursing home as an educator.

Nine months later, I was head-hunted to be an assistant director of nursing, one of three, for the Jewish for the Aged, a nine-unit facility. I was responsible for three units and Infection Control (IC) for the whole facility. HIV had recently been discovered and Universal Precautions was the standard safe care process. The facility knew nothing about universal precautions and the IC plan was very outdated. I joined every IC group I could find, went to as many conventions as I could, and learned. I was frequently told I had value, and the staff thanked me often. All of this was a boon to my self-worth and a glimmer of my sacred connection. Discovery continues.

Stop 6 discovery reflection – Wearing the victim persona, which is what lack of self-worth really is, is easy when in an emotional state. Blame shows up too, many times, as does shame. I've learned since then that shame means "should have already mastered everything," another core belief.

STOP 7 – Write, teach, and direct an Infection Control program for a new Kaiser Hospital in Santa Rosa, one hour north of San Francisco.

My daughter was very angry at me for taking her away from her friends and school. She was going into 8th grade at the time. I let her have choices that could help her adjust while I was adjusting. She loves Santa Rosa now and has settled with her husband, at least for now. Her best friend is here as well. For me, I was continuing to walk in discovery. We continued to go to Catholic Mass for at least six years, until she was out of high school. Then, it was her choice.

During this time, I discovered what it was like to have two teenagers in my home and teach four to drive. For two years when my daughter was 12 and 13, we had an exchange student stay with us for a year each. The student from Brazil was easy. The one from Germany pushed the boundaries. We all learned about how we show up and what may need to change. All my girls continued to be gifts to me. During this time, my food was a challenge as I felt so alone. Stuffing and hiding my feelings kept me from deep Divine connection.

Stop 7 discovery reflection – There are many blessings to be appreciated when I take the time to notice. Taking a conscious mindful breath slows me down, is a pause in the day, and brings me to the now. Now is where I can best connect with my body and with the divine, a gift of choice. My "girls" and their children continue to play a role in my life. My daughter remains my miracle.

STOP 8 – Travel called my name. My daughter was 24 and still at home.

I completed a master's degree and wanted to do something different but still within the Kaiser healthcare system. If she was not going to move out, I was. I found a job at Kaiser Hawaii and moved there. I felt so connected to Hawaii. Within a month, people I met thought I was "kamaaina" meaning local. I felt like I was home and belonged. This was great for my self-worth and opened me to divine energy. My daughter came to help me move in and to see where I was living. She did not like the feel of it. It was an apartment above a garage. I had to walk across an enclosed yard where the owner's dogs stayed to get to my car. The owner told me to notify her when I wanted to leave my apartment each day. I let her know the night before when I needed to leave. She was the hospital Infection Control (IC) nurse.

On my first day of work for orientation to my new position, I left the apartment and was walking across the fenced yard when one of the owner's dogs deeply bit me on my leg. I was blamed by the owner saying I did not notify her I was leaving, even though I informed her the previous evening. I had to be treated and was put on antibiotics. My body reacted to the antibiotics on day two with projectile vomiting during orientation with one of my new co-workers. My self-esteem was in the mire. I found a new apartment immediately. It was a true gift in a beautiful location closer to work with lovely people, where I finally experienced divine light.

I liked my job as a discharge planner and utilization review RN for the emergency room. The staff appreciated my perspective and energy. I felt at home and hoped to enjoy being in Hawaii for a long time. The IC nurse would not acknowledge me during the rest of my stay in Hawaii. I did not realize how upset I was until I looked back. Excess food continued to call me, but it was less pastries and more fruit.

Stop 8 discovery reflections – It's important to listen to the perceptions of ones that you love, especially when in an emotional state as I was with the move and separation from my daughter. It was time to cut the cord. It was both hard and necessary for her and for me.

STOP 9 – Another slice was taken out of my self-worth.

After eighteen months, my boss said I was not meeting their expectations when I worked my one weekend every six weeks doing discharge planning alone for in-patients on the hospital floors. It was a job that I did not do every day and was trained for it for only two days. The expectation was that I would complete the tasks as fast as those that did it full time, whereas I worked in a different job out of the emergency room (ER) full time except for that weekend. The patients, families, and staff that I worked with in the ER supported me, liked my energy and made me feel cared about. I was given the choice to resign or be fired. As much as I loved living in HI and my job, I knew that staying in that facility would not be wise. I chose to resign. I was given a month to find another job.

During my life in Hawaii, I traveled to many of the islands, experienced vortex energy, and was befriended. My friend and I explored spiritual energy in different ways and continue to have great discussions, even after 23 years. It turned out that we were buffers for each other as we were both experiencing job-related challenges.

Step 9 discovery reflection – Taking photographs of Hawaii's incredible beauty gave me a deep connection to earth energy and the divine—more than I realized. A deep lasting friendship is a gift to be nourished.

STOP 10 – I was back on the mainland for a job at Kaiser Vallejo. I worked 12-hour night shifts in the ER doing discharge planning and utilization review, which was the same job I did in HI. I missed the healing energy of Hawaii and my special friend.

Three wonderful years at Vallejo Kaiser Medical Facility was a boon to my self-image. For the first nine months I lived with a friend in Napa as my daughter, and her boyfriend were living in the Windsor condo. I was exposed to the 12-step way of life while living in Napa as my friend was in AA. It did not occur to me to connect the steps to my food issues. My 'care-taker core belief role' came to play as my AA friend was having physical and emotional issues. I again stuffed down my feelings to be there for her. This really did not serve either one of us.

I moved back to Windsor, the 55-mile commute one-way to Vallejo had been a struggle. Food and lack of conscious sacred connection continued to plague me even though I was home and was well-liked at work. My self-worth was slowly increasing. The search continued as my job moved back to Kaiser Santa Rosa after three years at Vallejo. I was so grateful for a 7-mile commute.

At Santa Rosa, I was the night shift house supervisor and in charge of the hospital and clinic next door. Staffing for the day shift, dealing with any issues that came up on the units or to do with the building, from broken pipes flooding the Central Sterile department, to a full hospital and emergency, all gave me a chance to practice soothing tools. My self-worth continued to expand. What was next?

Stop 10 discovery reflection – Walking in the Divine's glow of self-worth keeps the food addiction at bay. Using tools to walk in this light and soothe my emotions is a gift—one I wish to share with others. Mindful breathing, noticing and saying hello to what I am feeling are becoming second nature tools over time.

STOP 11 – This time included travel, PhD, and early retirement from Kaiser.

The travel bug has hit again now that my daughter is grown, and a friend asked if I would be her travel buddy. She is a brain energy specialist, an RN, and has a double PhD—one in spiritual ministry. We did overland travel in the British Isles, where I took beautiful photos. During this time, I completed a PhD in Human Services from Universal University, which has since closed.

Cruising with her became a passion of fun, brain stimulation, and discovery. Food wasn't such an issue as she is tiny and a vegetarian. I tended to eat as she did. I did get extra cookies when I went out alone, which stemmed from a core belief that if I hide my eating, no one will know. Brain fog on the reality of weight gain, tight clothes, and crumbs are all signs of overeating simple carbs.

Traveling to other countries stimulates the brain and leads to more discovery for me. Sitting on the bottom layer of the great pyramid at Giza and absorbing the incredible size and energy to create it, struck me deeply. Noticing how I was responding emotionally to the area, touched me to my toes as did the valley of the Kings, the Temple at Karnak, and Abu Simbel. The cruise up the Nile was lovely.

Cruising the Baltic Sea and visiting Estonia, Russia, Finland, and Sweden was our next adventure. In Finland, we decided to fly up to Lapland, which is above the Arctic Circle. We fed baby reindeer, shared local food, and watched an awesome show of local dancing. We were each blessed by the local shaman before our meal. We chose not to eat the reindeer stew after feeding "Bambi." Discovery here was how simply the people lived and enjoyed each other. It was somewhat magical.

Over the following years, we cruised to the top of Norway, again above the Arctic Circle, and out to the Canary Islands through the Straits of Gibraltar, with a stop in Casablanca. What a treat that was. We also enjoyed two or three different cruises in the Caribbean and the Gulf of Mexico. The cities that we stayed in and visited, the people that we experienced, and the photos I took were all a blessing for me. Hearing another language and seeing people smile and interact were gifts to my brain and my spirit. During our time on board the ship, she worked on her books and I gave her thoughts and edits. That she valued my suggestions was another self-worth boost for which I'm very grateful.

My PhD in Human Services was disallowed by the Federal Government Dept of Education after eight years of completion—worthiness drop. I ate to soothe the disappointment. I was not using the PhD for business. Having it gave my self-worth a boost.

After 24 plus years working with Kaiser in five different facilities, they offered me a buyout because I was one of their most expensive employees and close to retirement age. I was encouraged to take it by my financial planner. Because I had planned to work until 67 or 70, I didn't know what to do with my time. Three years of watching television, eating, doing some hobbies including photography, and taking some classes passed. Not the best way to live in retirement, I have found. I don't know if it would have been different if I had planned my retirement. I'll never know.

Stop 11 discovery reflection – Travel stimulates my brain and calms my food addiction. Retirement is a blessing if I walk in creativity and with the divine. Self-discovery, ongoing self-awareness, and photography continue to walk with me through retirement. Retirement is not about retiring from life. It *is* about changing my focus to living the most fulfilled life I can for the rest of it. There's so much yet to discover. Willing to travel unseen shores is the adventure of life.

STOP 12 – So much in this current stop which leads into my NOW—October 2023. This includes food and the 12 Steps, a Miracle Manifesting class, publishing a book, and this article for *Sacred Connection.*

I was introduced to a food-related 12-Step program in 2016 for which I am truly blessed and grateful. Working the steps, learning the spiritual principles, and living them one day at a time has changed my relationship with the Divine or my Dear One as I call my higher power. Wonder and ongoing discovery, releasing my self-will, and how I think about myself is a true gift from my Dear One. Honesty is step ones' spiritual principle, a gift every day. Being honest about how I feel, what I want to eat, and what I'm willing to surrender to the Divine has led to the feeling of peace and freedom at times. I remain active in multiple recovery meetings on zoom, which is a boon to meet people with food and body issues around the world. Spiritual tools that I use to assist me along my spiritual journey are meditation, journaling, making phone calls, living in the now, mindful breathing, being of service and so many more. Living a 12-Step spiritual life influences all areas of my life, even my relationship with food and food behaviors. My Dear One (Higher Power/the Divine) really does care about me and the choices I make each day.

The Miracle Manifesting classes expanded my self-worth and spiritual connection. It also encouraged me to create the book that I'd been thinking about for a year. The book was divinely led when I asked how I could get my photos out into the world to possibly help others. With help from many, my book *Discovery is Recovery: Brain, Emotion, and Spiritual Self-reflection Through the Creative Process*, a focused journal, came out in November of 2022. The focus is discovery of how honesty, hope, faith, courage, integrity, willingness, humility, self-discipline, love, perseverance, spiritual awareness, and service play in your life. It really is about living in the now.

The *Sacred Connections* workshop dropped into my life from the divine, after I asked my Dear One for opportunities to let women know I'm available to work with those who struggle with food or body image. I was asked to participate in the workshop, to speak on Discovery, and write this article for an anthology. These are amazing gifts to share who I am and how I can be of service in the world for my good, our good, and the highest good of all.

Stop 12 discovery reflection – For me, if "I **own** the **now** I've **won**, and I am **one** with my Dear One," I walk in gratitude. Sacred discovery is an ongoing journey. My attitude can make it fun or drudgery. It is truly my choice. Thus, I choose to dance with tough questions, challenging emotions or situations, and walk in the light of the spirit to the best of my ability one day at a time. My dream is to assist others to do the same, especially related to food, food behaviors and body image.

Thank you for sharing this time with me. It has been a gift in my discovery journey. I pray that it has shed light on your life journey of sacred discovery, especially any struggles with food. I would love to share in your journey if you choose to accept the one-hour gift session of discovery with me. Click on the link below or email me at **brenda@brendabalding.com**.

Blessings for you and your life journey,
Brenda

Alicia Power

Renowned Master Energy Healer and Spirit Communicator, Alicia Power is an educator of Healing Through The Soul Field, using Advanced Spirit Technology. After 40 years as a Spiritual Teacher Alicia has been trained by Senior Spirit Beings who reveal through her, accelerating knowledge and training for humanity. Alicia is a highly initiated soul that activates a person's consciousness evolution, soul wound history, and spiritual leadership. Alicia is a regular guest on consciousness tele-summits and podcasts, has authored over 20 transformational courses. Her YouTube channel has over 1.4 Million views.

7) CROWN — PRESENCE

THE SACRED ART OF LIFE

Giving Voice To Your Higher Self

by Alicia Power

FATHOMLESS DEPTH

I drank deeply from the stillness, the silence—of my mind.

The relief flooded through me as, like a tadpole urgently scrambling for the water's surface, I plunged deeper and deeper into the ocean of Presence.

This was my first time in this stillness. In this Presence.

The relief was of a soul, that had waited decades in a human body, finally touching "home."

I wanted to stay there, but my Indian Mahatma called us back—his eyes twinkling with delight as he gazed at my face, and the fathomless depth in my eyes. He laughed with joy.

She had found home.

That night as I walked to my lodging, I was drawn to gaze at the luminous leaves of a bush, glistening in the moonlight. And then it struck me—I was no longer tied to my thoughts, to my thinking mind.

I was different, anchored in my "silent witness"... separate from my thoughts. I was watching my thoughts chatter and comment. But "I"... was silent, still.

Simply Being—in the Presence of God Force.

Reconnected to that. Glued back into it.

I remember the first time I met someone who had been initiated into that Presence. Their eyes were deep, they had a space within them that wasn't touched by others opinions or jabs. I felt a Presence in them... quietly emanating.

That Presence is God Source.

This is the gift of being initiated into a 5,000 year lineage of meditation Avatars from India. I carry this Presence, anchored into it, until now, 40 years later.

THE MELTDOWN

Eight years after that first encounter with God Source, I was standing on a stage. I'd been called to give "Satsang" (a spiritual discourse) in front of the Indian Spiritual Master who'd flown across the world to assess potential teachers.

For the first time in my life, I was tongue-tied. (I'd performed on stages since the age of five, and I'd been "giving Satsang" several times a week for those eight years.)

I began speaking. Then, my world caved. And overwhelmed, I began to weep. In front of hundreds of people, and this true divine Master.

The grief was like a giant tidal wave, tossing me up, then stranding me on a beach for all to see.

To this day, I'm not sure what this grief pertained to. But it was existential. From the core of my soul.

Now looking back, perhaps my soul knew I had not attained the levels of consciousness, nor performed the "awakened soul path" I had been born to deliver and achieve.

It felt like I was on the wrong stage, moving in the wrong direction.

THE UPGRADE

Two years later I had my first Spiritual Healing energy session. An auric healing. The practitioner was a friend, deeply experienced, and I'd approached her knowing something needed to change.

I lay on the massage table, face up, clothed, as she placed her hands on my feet, behind my neck, lightly touching major joints like the knees, elbows, hips…

A warm soft energy flowed through me. Then, the relaxation moved deeper.

Suddenly, I felt my head moving slowly, insistently, to the right—then to the left.

I was not actively instigating this. But because I was so relaxed, my confusion was mixed with wonder.

What?… How?….

Everything about this felt comfortable. There was no fear or weirdness to this experience. Just strange, unfamiliar.

I quickly realized that the worlds of spirit were somehow able to control my body in that moment.

Then, instantly, I realized they were SHOWING me what they COULD do.

This moment was to be the beginning of a life of partnership—with Spirit Beings.

A partnership of them moving my body as an energy healer, them moving my thoughts as a speaker and teacher—of THEIR knowledge and work.

On the healing table, I sank further into a semi-conscious state with waves of gentle energy cocooning my body.

Twenty minutes had passed, and the soft vibrant cocoon suddenly peeled away.

I felt myself returning to full consciousness.

Slowly, I sat upright, and swung my legs off the massage table, dangling… trying to gather my thoughts.

I looked at my friend, the healer.

And once more…. an existential longing erupted from deep inside me. The longing finally had words:

"HELP me. I need to know WHO my SOUL is! I need to know its power. I need to BEGIN my true work as a SOUL!"

Within months of this urgent call to Spirit, I learned to dialogue two-way with multi-dimensional Spirit Mentors…

I read a simple inner focus exercise and the first time I tried it, to my amazement… a beloved Spirit Presence arrived.

And—we began our incredible life journey in partnership.

INFORMATION FLOW

I've read that for some committed meditation practitioners and monks, they discover from within the depths of their mental stillness, that psychic awareness begins to blossom like a flower.

They practice not making this their goal… however, their higher perception opens, begins to touch the fabric of Spirit, and this world then delivers gifts to these dedicated souls.

The reason I was able to perceive Spirit Beings' answers to my questions so quickly was because of the many years of a dedicated meditation practice.

My ability to focus inwards and intensely tune to the subtle realms allowed me to first FEEL, then interpret their responses—**not as logical thought, but as streams of transmissions.**

And this is the divine clue to spirit dialogue that I've now taught thousands of students for decades.

As a trained journalist, *I was beyond excited to begin dialoguing with intelligent Beings*—who were obviously reaching out to me. Nudging me to connect with them.

That first time, I asked into the "void": "What is your name?"

That first Being who approached me, their answer back to me was not what I expected! So, I didn't believe it. I kept repeating the question—but the answer stayed the same.

Eventually, I decided it didn't matter. So, I asked different types of questions, *to see if this connection was real.*

It was.

In those first attempts at spirit dialogue, an important realization ignited in me: *that what was trying to communicate with me was a Universe of specialist knowledge.*

On the other side of the veil, available to me, was infinite detail, science, wisdom, humor, vast consciousness that knows pretty much everything. It could travel into any particle of consciousness and matter, and report back.

Over the weeks, I patiently practiced, realizing it was I who was the concreted, numbed part of the potential conversation.

And through that practice, one word answers from Them turned into several word phrases... then sentences over weeks of daily practice.

I would write questions on paper, *then allow myself to FEEL the response flowing into my subconscious*—and without editing, write those responses down. Then once written—re-read them to comprehend the message.

THE SACRED ART

The Being who first connected with me—the most *Sacred Connection*—I subsequently came to know as a Grand Master Energy Healer. And a teacher of this specialist art.

For the next two years, He taught me detailed training in Spiritual Energy Healing, Etheric Energy Work.

Clients were attracted to receiving highly-skilled, **etheric surgery**, *because of my ability to blend my consciousness with this wonderful*

Mentor in Spirit, and the spirit teams of technicians that arrived to support each case.

I taught classes and workshops throughout Australia and New Zealand, in Energy Healing and Spirit Channeling.

At that time, 30 years ago, this healing work was already advanced because of my ability to translate and be an energetic extension of Master Healers.

I met and worked with many Master Spirit Beings who became my counselors and mentors.

Each healing client brought with them their own connected lineages of their personal Soul Spirit Mentors, who would make their presence known during energy healings.

And so, as I met these Beings, I would establish a relationship with them (just like human people), then channel their teachings in classes and groups.

I channeled the teachings of Egyptian gods and goddesses, Hawaiian goddesses, American Indian Chieftains and medicine women in Spirit, Ascended Masters like Jeshua, Mother Mary, and others, Archangels, Whale and Dolphin spirit wisdom, Galactic cosmic communities and many more.

This was the beginning of a long journey of expanding my belief systems, awakening to broader paradigms and knowledge of "how" the Spirit World worked.

And most importantly, I became steadfast and committed to bringing through the highest wisdom and healing for humanity.

This commitment follows me to this day.

LEARNING FROM SPIRIT

The depth and breadth of the story of my soul, its latent skills and talents, has been gently revealed over the three decades since then…

But what I walk with daily is a relentless knowledge that time is of the essence.

And that humanity does not have too much time left to mature into stewards of our Planet—before various scenarios move past tipping points into high gradient learning curves—for us humans.

And so my healing work morphed from working with individuals to group facilitation.

In these group trainings, I would meticulously allow Senior Advanced Spirit Mentors to lead us… into learnings and new cosmic awareness.

And also to lead us into the spirit realms—psychic healing spaces *where teams of High Light Spirit Healing Technicians would transmute soul wounds from our ancient soul history.*

Thus strengthening the hidden corners of our deepest soul selves.

And activating, triggering our ability to remember ourselves as beyond-human, as universal Souls.

Each group session was unique. Tailored to the souls participating. Tailored to the need of the moment.

And so my "work" became simply "following."

Following the recommendations of Senior Spirit Mentors when they invited me to form regular groups to travel into Spirit Realms with them for training and healing.

Following their revelations of *how the background Spirit Energies above all humans were affecting human dynamics*, decision-making—and evolving and devolving realities.

Following their revelations that THEY have an agenda, to deliver as much high authority Spirit Light into the subtle energy fields surrounding Earth and Humanity as possible—at this critical time, to activate change.

Following their strategy of keeping my personal aura clean from interfering low spirit energies, so that my own decision-making on a daily basis stays calm and elevated.

Following their recommendation to support many of my friends and family in the same way—so that my loved ones also remain clear and supported in their life.

Following an urgent call from them to meet with them daily to assess my personal energy system so that I remain able to connect with them.

Following their suggestion to teach others how to keep their own personal energy strong and clean, with tools and practices.

And most importantly, learning from them each day as to how the Spirit Worlds are interacting with humanity—sometimes in not such complementary ways.

ROGUE ACTORS

This awakening, that the Worlds of Spirit have rogue actors, and that humanity has an urgent need to be protected from these, came early in my work with my Spirit Mentors.

During client healings, the focus of the Spirit Healing Teams was to scan and travel along etheric (spirit) pathways that led to ancient soul wounds, moments of deep trauma.

These could be from previous incarnations, or from times spent as a soul before or between human lives.

As I watched the Spirit Technicians sense into these long tunnels of memory of a person's soul… they would come across fear. But a level of fear that was existential. Profound. Embedded into the very fabric of the Soul.

And around these points of trauma was the resonance of Shadow energy.

I've come to understand now that Shadow energy is a force beyond human comprehension.

This is part of the Spirit Dimensions that originally formed our universe.

Sometimes therapists refer to "shadow" as emotional wounds from childhood.

I'd like to gently reveal that this Shadow Force has super powers. And is not for humans to try and vanquish. It is beyond humans to try and comprehend.

The tackling of this shadow force is strictly for the realms of Spirit Light with the right qualifications.

And, having mentioned that—there is an urgent need for such "tackling."

WHY WE FEEL HURT

There comes a time in most people's lives where they unfortunately experience a moment—that hurts them. Whether in childhood, at school, at work, in relationships, within family dynamics.

I've come to understand, from my perspective and study inside the background spirit world, that these moments are instigated and guided by shadow Spirit Beings.

These Beings attach themselves to corners of our human aura, our multi-dimensional electro-magnetic field.

And they begin to influence either ourselves or those around us.

Their focus is to hurt, to cause harm, to cause doubt, uncertainty, chaos, and destructive circumstances.

They do this by embedding shadow frequency into specific parts of a human's auric system that relate to perception. Or mis-perception.

The person who is infected with such a shadow entity begins to develop unfounded stories in their mind, and project their feelings and aggravation onto another.

So, mis-perception (for me) is an instant indicator that a shadow Being is present, either in myself or another person.

Unfortunately, mis-perception is common throughout the human experience. And this helps us realize that shadow Beings are influencing many if not all of us humans to some degree.

My work as an energy healer is to remove these shadow Beings from a person's energy field.

So that people live their lives without fear and destructive behavior, so that they live their highest potential.

SPIRIT LOVE

Many years ago, I was working on a client's energy field, and saw a vast Being enter their field as I had my hands on their ankles.

I invited this Being to identify itself to me.

This is an important protocol for all energy healers so that they know the consciousness type of a new spirit being when it presents itself.

If you were in downtown New York and an unknown person stood in front of you, your immediate reaction would be to assess their energy—if they are safe to interact with, or not.

Exactly the same assessment needs to take place with Spirit Beings.

The Being turned to me and in response to my command to reveal its true essence, it showed itself to be a High-Level Egyptian God, the God Anubis.

It had arrived to add its benevolent healing resonance, and its specific mastery needed in this moment for this person's soul. It had melded with and interacted with the soul of the client in a long series of lifetimes—they knew each other well.

In this moment, this great Being wanted to support the activation of the client's soul to awaken faster, to remember itself as a great soul—faster.

This was a gift moment, and not to be taken lightly. I watched fascinated as Anubis sent its light intention and focus behind the heart center of this person. Time seemed to stand still—a long pause stretched the moment…

Then slowly there was movement, a sense that Anubis was pulling and jerking something that was stuck or concreted.

Then, freedom. The impression of a large hand holding a mass of energy, pulling it up through the layers of the energy field. And out—lifting this unsavory energy into the high light.

The client on the healing table yawned and stretched as if responding to the relief of a weight lifted.

Anubis turned to me and smiled, then instantly disappeared, merging back into its Higher Realm of Light.

This moment stayed with me through my decades of being a professional energy healer, because Anubis is a well-known Egyptian God in the Egyptian pantheon.

I was impressed by his fervent dedication to that soul, and his willingness to travel across time and space, through the layers of Spirit to reach this person in a key moment.

I've witnessed similar situations repeatedly over the years I worked with individual clients.

The worlds of spirit are incredibly passionate to uplift individuals they love. They will make enormous efforts to help and intervene on a person's behalf. Especially those they have had previous dealings with in other lifetimes and soul existences.

Relationships matter in the Worlds of Spirit.

They take "LOVE" seriously.

BRINGING IT TO THE PEOPLE

There are times when as a Spirit Communicator I wonder why there are not more everyday people chatting easily with their Spirit Mentors.

This ability seems normal and critical for fulfilling our purpose in our life.

These loving mentors are present, constantly around us.

Their level of knowledge, intelligence, skill, and commitment to us is beyond profound.

And yet, we in Western cultures have not been taught that Spirit Mentors are real, available, and watching and waiting for us to turn around and connect with them!

I've made it my life's mission to make this simple connection available to anyone who wants it.

I have an easy step by step, six module video course that teaches you how to listen, and how to interpret information flowing back to you from a Spirit Guide. Also how to focus quietly inside your mind so you sense your Spirit Mentor and use your logic to dialogue with them.

You can access that course HERE:

https://soulmentoring.me/course

The reason I am so passionate about this one single skill is because it changes your life.

Before the skill, there is a subliminal "wondering": "Am I performing at my optimum in my life?" "Am I missing something?" "Am I understanding myself fully?" "What is this life about anyway?" "Why do I feel I'm special—but everything in my life says I'm not!" "What truly is the purpose of MY life?" "WHO is my soul and what does it KNOW?"

CURRENCY OF LONGING

Once you make your life-changing *Sacred Connection* with your Guide, a Master Guide, the Guide who wants to mentor you into your inner freedom and power…

You then begin to meet with them regularly. To show up to your training sessions—and practice communicating. Practice communing in their Sacred Presence.

In those quiet moments, when you decide to FOCUS and call on your Guide, then FEEL them arriving to connect with you, your heart sings!

Because no longer are you alone—and wondering.

In those pin-drop, silent moments, when your Guide is sensing into your energy as they arrive, YOU have the prerogative to ASK.

For help.

For understanding of something that is bothering you.

This is a moment of LOVE and intimacy (because no one else KNOWS your SOUL like this Being).

This is a moment where YOU strive to receive the knowledge, insights, and wisdom from your Guide.

THIS is your *Sacred Connection* moment that resonates beyond this Life.

This moment, each time you connect deeply, OPENS ever more love, fruitfulness, wonder and relief to your human Self.

The relief that you are not alone. That the presence of your Guides walk with you. They will never leave you. That "door" is always open.

However, your effort and "striving" is the key.

Because if this divine Connection fades into the hurry and noise of your life, and you don't "tend" to it, your Guide will gently STEP BACK and wait, until YOU quiet, and turn to them.

So, noticing your need, your longing, your deep soul yearning is key.

Because that, dear reader, is the glue, the ultimate drive of optimizing your lifetime.

I am describing my own journey to **fulfillment as a soul.** As you read, you may feel a longing to activate this critical opportunity for yourself.

The reason? Without the caring presence of your Guides throughout life's challenges, your journey could move through difficulties that otherwise may be unnecessary.

STEWARDSHIP

Many years ago, I realized that humanity needed help.

Brave decision-making, levels of spiritual awareness, and global stewardship are sorely lacking.

And that is why I'm writing this short summary of my personal story.

Because as a trained journalist and writer, I had a curiosity coupled with the ability to step back and observe the big picture—then translate that into normal language and concepts.

Also, my parents taught me to innovate, to be creative, to trust myself, to speak up, and to honor my own perception.

I was part of a large musical family, where we all learned classical instruments and played together in quartets and musical groups.

We learned that collaborating in groups, creating a sublime group harmony, and the pristine architecture of classical compositions were to be respected.

Beauty and art were to be respected. The best of humanity was to be respected and encouraged.

I feel it is that sentiment that underlies the reason I teach direct dialogue with Spirit Mentors.

To make that connection conscious and deliberate.

Because I witness that the mentoring worlds of Spirit are often the true underlying wellspring of visionary INSPIRATION birthing from within us humans.

It is they who are touching our souls, uplifting our hearts—quietly from behind the veil.

Whether that is art, hope, innovation, teaching, or decision-making.

Inspiring us. Teaching us. Guiding us.

We need this up-leveling mentoring—urgently.

We need help with guiding our human family into a higher level of understanding:

- That we are all together in a short playground moment.
- That this short life is to be lived in harmony and equanimity
- That we have a responsibility to our collective global family—their welfare, their safety, their wellbeing.
- That Planet Earth is a living Being, an ecosystem that is incredibly sensitive to over-consumption and destructive industrialized practices.
- That we as humans are like children who've consumed too much sugar and are having tantrums!
- That we are not alone in this universe, and that help is well and truly available at an instant.

AN OPTIMIZED LIFE

I've learned that "living your life optimally" doesn't need to be a driven chore or even a strong focus.

Your days can unfold with you simply FOLLOWING your inner Guidance.

Because together with your ability to dialogue with your Spirit Mentor, you can immediately receive accurate prompts, as to what priorities need to be implemented each day. (This is my experience.)

Priorities could be self-caring, exercising, eating healthy foods, and having rest and ease.

Counter-intuitively, all these can (under guidance from your Mentor) *MOVE you forward toward your destiny in this life.*

Because through this "soft focus" your Spirit Mentor WILL "guide" you into a moment of discovery, self-expansion, and contribution.

As you sense into your Guidance each day, or at ANY moment in your life, you can receive clear gentle prompts of where to put your attention and what needs to be attended to.

Whether that is a writing project, to connect with someone who can broaden your horizons in skills or networking, or to read something that triggers a new idea or project…

ALL these moments are guided carefully so that YOU win this game of optimizing this life.

It is truly up to you to foster this sensitivity, this realization that you are not alone—at any moment.

And that this sacred partnership is real, tangible, and an invaluable treasure as you walk this life.

You may find your striving for fulfillment is successful *because* you are listening to prompts and suggestions.

However, a gentle reminder: when it comes to business dealings, creating income-producing projects, YOU are the one that needs to move through up-skilling, step-by-step *so your competency and comprehension increases.*

Magic happens when you know the frameworks, make the effort to learn skills, AND work with Spirit Guidance for ideas, creativity, AND motivation! (All of which they eagerly support us with!)

YOUR SOUL'S AGENDA

As a teenager, and in my early 20's, I learned that no one outside of you really knows what is happening in your private heart.

Even your most beloved family members.

That world inside you is so personal, sometimes simply motivated to succeed in this life. Or to survive, to contribute, and to be loved.

There are many urgent hidden drivers that remain unconscious even to you, as you move through your life.

However, underneath all of them is one overarching driver…

The longing for fulfillment.

You may love being with friends and family. You may love fitness, art, books, or conversations. All of these are elements to a fulfilled life.

Yet your deepest need that longs to be fulfilled, is to meet your own soul, and your soul mentors, who wait until you turn to them deliberately.

And then, to converse with them.

Your logical mind may never have thought about this!

But beyond this life, THIS is your longing: *To reunite with the GREATER, higher you, and your greater soul family above and beyond this short life.*

This divine persistent longing for me was never understood by my conscious mind.

It was simply an itch that couldn't be scratched!

Now, looking back over my life, I can see a continuous thread right from those early years of learning to meditate. Actually, from moments in childhood when "God" was already something I longed for.

As humans, our lives can travel through tough times. Times when you wonder if you'll survive emotionally, psychologically, and even perhaps physically.

Yet through these times, if you can continue to "hope," to keep a spark alive somewhere deep down, that "this too shall pass"... **a determination may arise and build, through those experiences...**

Until that determination finds the path into soul fulfillment.

And so, this short chapter may spark that recognition in you.

That soul fulfillment is really all you want beyond it all.

And if, and when, it feels the right time for you, **your spirit mentors are right behind you. Actually walking with you, guiding you along this seeking path.**

You'll feel the correctness of finally turning within, to MEET your sacred Spirit Tutors, and have CONVERSATIONS with those that see your soul.

That love you fervently, passionately, and eternally.

And those conversations will be poignant, urgent, focused, and **hungry for clarity on what it takes to awaken your mind to your soul's unique greatness.**

So that YOU fulfill your soul's agenda, the reason your soul incarnated in this human lifetime.

To sign up for inspiration in your inbox from Alicia, go here: https://soulmentoring.me/list

To experience training in dialoguing with your guide, go here: https://soulmentoring.me/tutor

Visit me at my website: https://soulmentoring.com

Printed in the USA
CPSIA information can be obtained
at www.ICGtesting.com
JSHW070913241223
54129JS00013B/58

9 781959 608622